257

"*Taste*, accompanied by *Rural Simplicity*, pointing to one of the most beautiful scenes this island can boast, viz. the Lake of Windermere."

from Plaw's *Rural Architecture*, 1794

ENJOYING THE LAKES

From Post-chaise to National Park

BY

EDMUND W. HODGE

OLIVER AND BOYD

EDINBURGH: TWEEDDALE COURT

LONDON: 39A WELBECK STREET, W.I.

FIRST PUBLISHED . . 1957

PRINTED IN GREAT BRITAIN BY
T. AND A. CONSTABLE LTD., EDINBURGH, FOR
OLIVER AND BOYD LTD., EDINBURGH

FOR KENNETH BELL

AND ALSO

FOR HERBERT BELL

CONTENTS

CONTENTS

ILLUSTRATIONS

CHAPTER I

THE KNOWLEDGE OF GOOD AND EVIL

THE PURPOSE of this book is to trace the development of the appreciation of our mountain scenery, as exampled in that of the Lake District, and also its relation to contemporary ideas in other fields, such as those of art, fashion, social history and even politics. With a historical subject, it is often difficult to know where to draw the boundaries of one's period. We all remember the history-books of our schooldays, in which costume history (as one may call it) with its well-marshalled evidence and clear issues, and its air of being competently produced for the stage on correct principles of art, peters out somewhere about the date when the Archbishop of Canterbury made his early morning call on the girl-queen Victoria. There was something about William IV and the era of stove-pipe trousers which was repugnant to the Muse, although later episodes like those of Lucknow, Omdurman, and even Lady-smith seemed still compatible with dramatic treatment. But in truth an uneasy interregnum lay between the long ages about which, fortunately for artistic presentation and even for the practice of scholarship, we could never know all; and our own times about which we, however young and un-schooled, somehow knew too much. Somewhere between the two there was always a blind spot, as at the point where a lens first begins to give a reversed image, or like a sound barrier, which nobody seemed to care to write through. Then again, Good Tendencies had a way of slowly broaden-ing down from precedent to platitude, until merged at last in the estuarine flatness of general acceptance. If one had been writing in 1850, one would have said this was what had happened to discriminatory taste for scenery. But, as the nineteenth century closed, it renewed its impetus, and

offered us a strong sporting finish with the establishment of
National Parks. Now, therefore, is a time for stocktaking.

The problem of a starting-point is perhaps a little more
difficult. The scholarly method is, of course, to begin exactly
where the evidence begins, but to the philosophical spirit
this is not satisfying. The need is felt of a satisfying overall
picture, at a given date, but very often the evidence may not
be sufficient to provide one. To adopt the simple method of
beginning where the written records begin may seem to
amount to the assumption that in the days when people did
not write about their acts and feelings, things either did not
happen or were not felt, or at least were not significant, and
results in notes for a history, rather than a history itself. We
will not need, however, to make an assumption as bland as
this. One may, for example, go back to the dark ages for
one's starting-point, gleaning from the sparse *obiter dicta* of
(necessarily) monkish writers such fragments of doctrinal
implication or gossipy legend as may seem to indicate an
attitude to mountain scenery. Thus it has been suggested
that mountains, at least some of the Alpine ones, were
generally thought to be the resort of devils, lost souls or
dragons. Churchmen, then the articulate part of the community, inclined to distrust them because things were apt
to take place in their recesses, by grove and fountain, over
which it was not easy to invigilate—witchcraft and idolatry,
the sins of the flesh and the stubborn relics of pagan faiths.
No doubt there is something in this, but it need not be
accepted as an account of the attitude of mediaeval people
generally.

The foregoing no doubt presupposes mountains on a
rather grander scale than we have them in England. In the
case of the Lake District, we are much more concerned with
the sheep-farming monks of the great Abbey of Furness.
Those who worship the awful majesty of mountains should
remember that through most of history, and especially in
earlier times, it is woods which have been in preference
regarded as the objects of dread, or of imagination; from the

those few local poems compared with his language in describing objects with which his position in life allowed him to be familiar.'

Organised sentiment therefore it is, rather than native sensibility, which is our theme, although it is useful to return from time to time to the latter, as a control or measuring-rod for the former. It is this that makes the question of starting-point so much easier to handle, since a sentimental picture of this kind is an affair for outsiders, for the articulate, for townsmen; and the social and other changes which brought the interest of these classes of people to bear upon the charms of Lake District and other similar scenery were comparatively rapid, recent and easily traceable.

So far as the art of painting was concerned (if we may widen our field of view somewhat beyond Britain), up till the sixteenth century, mountain scenery by no means came amiss to the innocent eye. The human drama, naturally enough, occupies the centre of interest. The pious donor, as is fitting, wears his best suit of armour, every detail of its costly inlay admiringly depicted. His rich acres, his castle on its picturesque crag, his family, are lovingly enumerated. Unstained by tedious naturalism, unfenced by officialdom, the good Kings from the East, unselfconscious and accessible to all, lay their rich and elaborate gifts by the manger, right next to the well-known instruments of simple husbandry. The heavenly host, sometimes even the Father Himself, looks down on it all, clear beyond peradventure to the eye of faith, for do not the stars in their courses, the knight in his pride, the priest, the poor man at his labour, the springing crops, the domestic beasts, all alike have their place by His permission in the great scheme of Creation? But there too, surprisingly often, are introduced mountains; far too often, as I think, for anyone to claim that they were either unloved or unknown. Again, natural features, especially mountains, are not usually depicted with much detail in these old pictures, and of course there is no pedantry about scale, any more than there is in the depiction of buildings or even people. Usually the fragment of mountain landscape is introduced merely as one more item in the inventory of the possessions of the artist's patron. But now and again a Hans Leu (of Zürich, d. 1531) cannot resist giving us a picture in which the saint in the foreground seems but the excuse for the mountain scene in the background. Or a Joachim Patinir, also working in the early years of the sixteenth century, shows that he saw landscape as such, not merely as a random collection of distant natural features. The crags in these old pictures are perhaps not like our idea of crags. But before we dissent, we ought no doubt to be familiar with the kind of mountain countryside with which the artist was familiar. It is of course the eye for landscape features as a whole which is important, for mountains, even for our purposes, are no more than a part of landscape. What is significant is that the mediaeval artist and his patron, over-masteringly intent on the issues of the soul's salvation or the concerns of earthly state, which provided the motive for the painting, should have had attention left in any degree at all for natural scenery. I believe that what is missing from mediaeval pictures in this respect is not so much awareness of nature either in detail or in general, but self-conscious selectiveness.

At length, with increasing sophistication, both in philosophy and in the craft of painting, the unitary conception of life burst at the seams. Painters differentiated their material more and more. Sitters consented to be shown in the actual lighting and in the commonplace activities of the moment, no longer *sub specie aeternitatis*. It became possible for moods to be isolated: the Laughing Cavalier must not be supposed to have spent his whole life in laughter. Conscious 'tastes' now become possible, something one may put on or off at will, like a hat. The pictures of the interiors of bourgeois dwellings and the landscapes of the Netherlands are no longer dependent on the human figures in them; they speak directly to us. If mountains do not figure very much at first, this is more an accident of nationality and location than anything: the way to mountain sentiment is nevertheless wide open. The so-reasonable objections of the feudalist, the moralist, the humanist, the practical agriculturalist are overruled as not relevant. Sentimentality has been defined as the cultivation of feeling for its own sake; for this, the fragmentation of the mental field is a prerequisite. The roving picturesque eye is set free, and, as it happens most conveniently, the top quarter of the canvas at the same time is no longer required for its ancient supernatural tenants—*levabo oculos, unde auxilium meum?*

Once granted the principle of picturesqueness, it is quite as easy to make a landscape out of an arrangement of skylines or out of moorland scenery, as out of canals and willows; it only requires a little more walking—so the mountains are pressed into service more and more. The religion of nature, though perhaps not incompatible with more conventional or more spiritual religion, is certainly particularly congenial to those who for one reason or another have little disposition towards the other kinds.

Parallel with changes in the arts and in feeling, came the growth of national and foreign trade and power and the consequent increase of wealth and the immense growth of the towns, with more traffic and travel, better roads, better inns. More people had more money and, even more important, more social freedom to form tastes for this or that. The townsmen and the countrymen alike became more civilised, more articulate, more literate, even though urbanisation, until the age of the motor car, was in some ways pushing them further apart.

Right down to the present day, therefore, the writing about the Lake District tends to belong to one of two distinct streams. There is the one arising from the countryman's intimate knowledge, and the other springing from the personal discovery, often nostalgic in feeling, of the townsman. It is the latter group that starts with the advantages, frequently carrying the heavier armament of professional talent, or a sharper spearhead of feeling; but where there

B

is not something like this to rely on, this group includes by far the worst. With the growth of the two factors I have mentioned, sentimental selectivity and social development towards urbanisation, the scene is set for the literary-aesthetic appreciation of mountain scenery.

CHAPTER II

JACOBEAN AND HANOVERIAN

HAVING CAUTIONED THE READER, rather heavily perhaps, against some of the pitfalls of a narrowly documentary approach even to an essentially literary subject, we must now ourselves follow that method, taking in our stride, just as they may happen to come, the men of original perception and the men of theories, the journalists and the escapists, the over-emphatic poseurs and the tersely practical.

In relying on documentary or biographical material in tracing the beginnings of a taste for mountain scenery, one is apt to feel the insignificance of the individual accounts utilised. Here perhaps an obscure clergyman, in the course of a book of entirely different subject-matter and purpose, obliges with a few words handy for the subject of one's interest; here one finds a footloose eccentric whose real object in travel was horse-exercise and gastronomic novelty. These are duly canonised as prophets of a cult they would have been surprised to hear of. When one finds a work addressed directly to the subject, and at the same time an unmistakable aristocrat of literature, it is indeed a treasure; but one may still be sceptical about its contemporary influence, its representative character or even its sincerity. Or, for example, one finds Great Gable shown for the first time on a map; but what one has to remember is that this is not so much an event in the story of the mountain, which for a thousand years had been familiar by name and face to considerable numbers of people, as a symptom of the spread of popular map-publishing.

Did the organisation of tourist interests in the Lake District really spring suddenly into existence because a donnish recluse made a three weeks' carriage tour there?

Again, one can make an imposing list of great names directly encountered in one's researches, without necessarily admitting that their poetic depth and force was matched by their originality or acuteness as commentators on landscape. The wider considerations mentioned in the last chapter may have been very sketchily dealt with there, but at least the background awareness of them helps to keep the unavoidable personalities in better proportion.

A convenient (if arbitrary) starting-point for tracing the growth of aesthetic ideas about our British mountains is in Camden's *Britannia*. An Elizabethan, he was unembarrassed and versatile in his interests, and unaffectedly fanciful and appreciative. Gay imaginative touches in his book jostle with agricultural information and family history: he seems something like the native Gothic outlook of England made articulate by the impact of the Renaissance, but not yet affected by the eighteenth-century ideas labelled respectively 'moral', 'sentimental', 'romantick', 'philosophick', and so on. Where Camden has a model, it is a classical one. Thus Ingleborough is 'The Highest of our Appennine'. One does not find in Camden any sign of exaggerated dread of mountains, or any feeling that they constitute an impassable barrier. As an amateur of scenery, he is perfectly impartial between mountains and other natural features, such as rivers. Thus, while the small Lancashire river Douglas 'creepeth and stealeth along quietly', the Ribble comes 'with a quick and hasty stream out of the hills in Yorkshire, by three exceeding high mountains, Ingleborough hill at the spring head, which I wondered at to see how it ascendeth as it were by degrees with a huge and mighty ridge westward and at the furthest end mounteth up into the air as if another hill were set upon the head of it', and so on.

Of Cumberland he writes:

Although it be somewhat with the coldest, as lying farre North, and seemeth by reason of hilles, yet for the variety thereof it smileth upon the beholders, and giveth contentment to as many as travaile it. For, after the rockes bunching out, the mountains standing thick together,

NATURE IN THE MID-EIGHTEENTH CENTURY

Design by Bentley from the first edition of Thomas Gray's *Odes*, 1766

SEVENTEENTH CENTURY RUSTICITY

from Blaeu's *Map of Cumberland*, 1648

PART OF CHRISTOPHER SAXTON'S WESTMORLAND, 1607

Scale: 1 inch=1 mile

rich of mettal mines, and betweene them great meeres stored with all kinds of wild fouls, you come to pretty hills for good pasturage and well replenished with flocks of sheep, beneath which again you meet with goodly plaines spreading out a great way, yeelding corne sufficiently.

Farther on, Camden speaks of the Roman fort at Hardknott, 'an high steep mountain, in the top whereof were discovered of late huge stones and foundations of a castle, not without great wonder, considering it is so steep and upright, that one can hardly ascend up to it': a fair observation, if he is speaking (as he reasonably would, in the case of a habitation) of getting up to it with vehicles and so on, in the way of ordinary convenience. Camden, in fact, nearly always speaks not unkindly of mountains. Even those of Ross-shire are 'huge swelling mountains bearing their heads aloft . . . most truly preservers of snow'. One could not blame anyone travelling among the latter, in weather not of his own choosing, who should allow some words harsher than this to fall from him.

Others were more practical-minded than Camden. As was natural in one who had risen in the world, Sir Daniel Fleming's mind, when he wrote his description of Cumberland (1671), ran on the dignity of his ancestral descent, and on the long records of the ownership of land. From a physical point of view, Wasdale to him was 'a fforest well stocked with dear', neither less nor more. The Honourable Celia Fiennes, who toured England in the reign of William and Mary, must have been a good sensible lady interested in all sorts of sensations, but not carrying her head in the clouds. Seeing Windermere 'full of little hills or isles', she took boat to Belle Isle (then plain 'Householm'), viewed its arrangement and its crops, and came back to more serious business: 'Mrs. Rowlandson, she does pott up the Charr ffish the best of any in the country: I was curious to have some and bespoke some of her.'

But the 'native' attitude towards mountains, matter-of-fact though often by no means unadorned with imagination, was to give place. The opinion that mountains were merely 'horrid' (that is, sensational or shocking), or 'disgusting' (that is, distasteful), is characteristic of the Age of Reason, corresponding closely with the unfashionableness of Gothic architecture. It was that expressed by Defoe, by Addison, by Bishop Burnet. Leslie Stephen described it well; but it has attracted rather too much attention, if it is regarded as the general attitude of our forefathers.

The general frame of mind upon which rested this attitude towards scenery rapidly became predominant in England at the Restoration, and did not begin to ebb much before the middle of the eighteenth century. Like all others, it found its corresponding expression in all the interests of life, from theology to landscape gardening. At the heart of the style, with its massive porticoes and buxom cherubs, is the rejoicing in the rebirth of a gracious idealised antiquity, the comparative triumph of order, reasonableness, and plenty, all too scarce in the familiar world of war, particularism and sectarian fanaticism, bad roads and snowy mountains. There is no need to enlarge here on this climate of opinion, only to note, in regard to mountain scenery, its Cumbrian application, in a little book on the minerals of the county, by Thomas Robinson, the Rector of Ouseby, published in 1709. While applying the common criteria of his time, he contrives to avoid condemning the familiar features of his northern landscape, as a southerner might have done:

Some of our late theorists . . . seem to be of opinion that the ante-diluvian earth was mathematically round, without mountains hills or valleys, as if these exuberances of its surface, like warts and wens, were the deformities of it. But if these new theorists had considered that God had made nothing in vain, but to wise ends, and the best of purposes though our dark intellect is not able fully to comprehend them, they would have been convinced of their mistake. These high and lofty mountains do not only contribute to the entertainment of our visive faculty, with most curious and delightful landskips, but present us with a set of vegetables peculiar to their cold and elevated soil, and most proper and agreeable with the hot natures of sheep and other creatures bred upon them. . . .

They also, he points out, serve to distribute rainfall.

Thousands of southern Englishmen no doubt were introduced to the scenery of Northern England, as to something new in nature, whilst serving in the Hanoverian army during the campaign of 1745 against the Highland rebels. But of these, only one or two seem to have left such a narrative as can be described as 'Tour'. It is to such as the anonymous 'Volunteer' that one has to look for what the middle-class Georgian really thought about mountains: what impression these made on an open mind, not insensitive but, in the circumstances, not inclined to sentiment or fine writing. Apparently a regular officer, seasoned in many lands, he was so new to our English fells, or expected his readers to be so, that he found it necessary to describe even a common Westmorland beck: 'These rivers are quite different from those in the Southern parts of England . . . through the whole course the stream is filled with mighty rock-stones; the sides generally lined with a firm rock. . . .' In all the circumstances of a campaign in December and January (unaccustomed and often scant food, hardship, and even losing part of his lip by frostbite) the degree of his appreciation of scenery does him great credit. From the churchyard at Kirkby Lonsdale 'we have a most entertaining prospect of the snowy mountains, at a vast distance, and the beautiful course of the River Lune, in a valley far beneath us'.

His detachment's way lay from Kendal to Kirkby Stephen 'over continued high mountains covered with snow. We frequently come to valleys, which with great fear and danger we descend, they being so very steep. This was the most strange journey I ever made. . . . These strange and wonderful varieties makes the time pass away agreeably enough, till my foundation and spirits begin to sink with fatigue.' His diction is, to our ears, oddly stiff: fir woods are 'mighty solitary and amusing and are the only artificial beauty of these mountainous places', and 'afford an entertaining scene to the wearied traveller'. He conceived a genuine feeling for the becks, and often mentions them. At the descent of each weary moor, he says, one is 'sure of

meeting a most agreeable view, with noisy purling streams
. . . which cascade, together with its noise, gives a person
disposed to solitude, a most agreeable harmony, but with all
these pleasing varieties, yet we endure great fatigue and
hunger'.

Surely the man who could write thus, in a snowy
December, perhaps after a bivouac in the open following on
a succession of hard days, had in him a susceptibility to
nature as rare in our age as in his! After this, one can be
generously sympathetic at finding him troubled by the
common vertigo or bathyphobia of the plainsman: 'a most
surprising hole, or small valley' the Devil's Beef Tub, near
Moffat, frightful to look down, being so exceeding steep
and deep, that one would think it extream dangerous to
descend'. Later 'one of the rebels ran down here, when
coming prisoner to Carlisle, and' (one is hardly surprised)
'made his escape'. From Inverness to Fort Augustus: 'We
travel through a road made with the greatest difficulty, by
blowing monstrous rocks, which in many places hang
stooping over passengers, and higher than houses, so that it
is a little frightful to pass by them.'

It is noticeable if hardly surprising in the circumstances
that our author's taste for mountain scenery rather decreases
than gains by continued acquaintance, for after months in
garrison at Fort Augustus he writes, referring to the
diversions of the troops:

It was necessary to entertain life in this manner, otherwise by the
constant view of mountains surrounding us, we should have been
affected with hypochondriacal melancholy . . . constantly black skies,
and rusty-looking, rocky, mountains, attended with misty rains and
cutting winds with violent streams of water rolling down from every
part of the mountains.

With the defeat of the rebellion of 1745, small as had been
in fact its chance of success, an intangible but heavy load
seems to be lifted from the national life. The nation having
been compelled, in face of an enemy, to act on a definite
political choice, the habit of bitter (and latterly rather

meaningless) party strife about issues which had come down from the seventeenth century was to be felt as an anachronism. No longer did the progressive townsman and the small country squire see in each other, the one a covert Jacobite rebel and sottish petty tyrant, and the other an upstart who had battened on the decay of all that was honest and basic in the national life. The people at large, having thus regained a measure of self-respect, had more attention to spare for new ideas, and for the arts and graces of life. A long period of peace and increase of trade had indeed supplied the material means for advance, and for the spirit of adventure. Metropolitan manners being less suspect in the provinces, and provincial inns and roads somewhat bettered, travel began to be for the first time reasonably attractive.

CHAPTER III

MAPS AND ROADS

IT WAS LATE in the sixteenth century before any attempt was made towards a general map survey of England. Such few small-scale maps as there had been were not built up from actual surveys, which scarcely existed, but had taken as their basis the rough outline furnished by the part of Ptolemy's map relating to Britain, and had proceeded by the correction of a few obvious deficiencies here and there, or the insertion of a few places of interest to the special purpose for which the map was required.

Under the Tudors, the desire of a strong government for closer administrative control made a better map needful. A set of sketch maps of English counties for the personal use of the first Lord Burghley shows nothing at all but rivers and the names of the local magistracy and gentry—against the names of some of whom is set, rather ominously, a cross.

Accordingly in 1574 Christopher Saxton, who had commenced his career in one of the great official households, set out, no doubt with official encouragement, on a perambulation of England. By 1577 he had completed a survey which was a remarkable effort for a pioneer, although necessarily very rough.

There is almost no direct evidence of the way he went to work; that is, apart from the evidence afforded by his maps. These, forming the first atlas of English counties ever published, were issued in 1579, and smaller reprints of them were used in the editions of Camden's *Britannia*, from 1607 onwards to 1695.

The earliest natural features to attract the attention of the map-maker and topographer were the rivers. Their valleys were the seats of cultivation, and they were at once highways and the most obvious kind of natural obstacle. Consequently,

interest, even of a literary sort, gathered around them
hundreds of years before the very existence of mountains
excited any remark. It is rivers alone which appear in the
county maps of Drayton's *Polyolbion* (1622). The maps of
Saxton and of others a long while after are only thinly be-
sprinkled with mountains, inserted in the most empirical way
and without any consistency at all. 'Skiddaw Hill' and
'Helvillon Hill' are the only ones, in the Lakes, mentioned
by their individual names. The same semi-pictorial symbols
as do duty for these serve also for road summits, such as
'Shire-stones upon Wrynose' and an unnamed one, intended
no doubt for Honister Hause, which fills the gap between
the headwaters of Buttermere and Borrowdale. Troutbeck
village is set on the top of another such marking. Another
appears in South Westmorland as a sort of compromise
between the positions of Scout Scar and Warton Crag, and
there are a few more. No distinction is made as to height,
and no representation of profile is attempted. Farleton Fell,
near Carnforth, so conspicuous from the main road, is
indeed shown a good deal bigger than 'Helvillon', no doubt
because of its prominence as a landmark.

Prominence in the landscape was no doubt the criterion
of the rhyme quoted in Camden:

> Ingleboro, Pendle and Penyghent
> The highest hills between Scotland and Trent.

But it is only fair to Camden to mention that he quotes in
the same work another local variant:

> Skiddaw, Helvillon, and Casticand,*
> The highest hills in all England.

On a map of 1771, Ingleborough is stated to be 1760 yards
high, Penyghent 1740 and Pendle 1560 yards. This suggests
that the map-maker was anxious to do honour at the same
time to one of Yorkshire's finest peaks, and to the English
statute mile, by making the number of yards in each equal.

From the earliest maps onwards private parks are

---

* Casticand=Catstycam, a peak of Helvellyn.

indicated, but quite as much, one feels, on account of the political or magisterial importance of their owners as for their geographic interest. Conventionalised trees are frequently shown in parks and in other regions described as forests, like Copeland Forest to the north of Wastwater, but are not to be taken as meaning that the places so marked had in fact many, or any, trees. The primary notion of 'park' is an enclosure, and of 'forest' an area of waste, available for hunting, with trees only incidentally in either.

The liberal display of heraldry on seventeenth-century maps and of the names of the owners of the estates (who would be largely identical with the magistracy) on eighteenth-century ones, was then of vastly more practical importance even to the private traveller than now. Map-making, on the county scale at least, owed its birth rather to political considerations than to any disinterested curiosity about natural phenomena; and the official Heralds, whose business it was in Tudor times to make their own local visitations, were sometimes inclined to regard the earlier map-makers as interlopers or quacks in their own profession.

Of course no roads appear at first, since until the turnpike era roads were almost as much to be avoided for their badness as followed. On the larger scale maps it is possible to see from the dotted-line boundaries of roads, that they were, not nearly so much as now, merely narrow strips between enclosed properties. The traveller often had cause to rejoice when he was free to pick his own way across a common or waste, instead of being confined to the deep ruts or morass. But the position of bridges is, from the first, set down with accuracy and completeness second to those of no other feature.

The first *Road Book of England*, Ogilby's, was published in 1675; and the maps in the editions of Camden from 1695 onwards show (on the Westmorland but not on the Cumberland map) a few of the main roads: Lancaster to Carlisle, Shap by Tebay to Kendal, Penrith to Ambleside over Dunmail Raise.

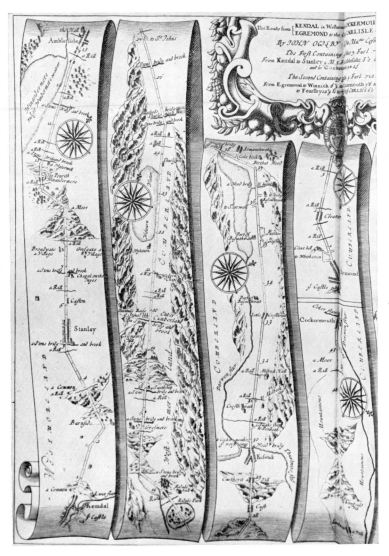

THE KENDAL TO COCKERMOUTH ROAD

from Ogilby's *Britannia*, 1675

PART OF A NEW MAP OF CUMBERLAND AND WESTMORLAND

Actual Scale

by Bowles and Sayer, 1760

Blaeu's maps (1645) represent the high-water mark of artistic cartography. All the maps of the sixteenth and seventeenth centuries—those already mentioned as well as Speed's (1610) and Jansen's (1646)—have a strong family resemblance and all fundamentally rest on Saxton's survey.

In the eighteenth-century maps a change is felt, but in some ways scarcely for the better. Detail was multiplied but accuracy (except for a better coastline) little improved. From about 1750 onwards some very prolific London publishers and engravers: Bowles, Sayers, Carrington, Kitchen and Bowen, forming often-changing partnerships or competitive firms, produced good and interesting maps.

Names are abundant and mines and objects of general rather than merely geographical interest are marked. This title is typical: 'A New Map of the Counties of Cumberland and Westmoreland divided into their respective Wards; From the best surverys and intelligences; Illustrated with historical extracts relative to Natural History Produce Trade and Manufacturers; shewing also the Rectories and Vicarages; with various other improvements.'* This is far from the simple dignity of the seventeenth century with its 'Cumbria Comitatus vulgo Cumberland'.

The representation of mountains on such maps as Bowles' and Sayers', though still immensely far from accuracy or even from fair approximation, begins to bear witness of revision by many hands, and of attempt to distinguish between big and little ones with less regard to mere prominence, and to fix the position and shape of the areas of high ground. No heights are yet shown, and contemporary estimates of these are absurdly erroneous. Lakes fare much better, but are a good deal mangled. The number and position of their islands are fixed rather upon decorative considerations than by regard to fact. It is hard to see why it should have been at all difficult to find, by survey, the shape of an inland lake, whatever may have been the case with a coastline. But the general impression one gets from

* Bowles' and Sayers' large folio map of 1760 from the Royal English Atlas.

the maps of the middle of the eighteenth century is that they were drawn in some London garret, no doubt by capable and conscientious draughtsmen (and perhaps from the best available partial surveys or estate maps, which must have been getting commoner by this time), but that, being produced primarily to hit the market, they were not based on adequate survey and were rather below what one would expect from the period.

It was well known, no doubt, that the Cumbrian hills must be familiar to the rude fellows who herded beasts or pursued game among them,* but there is not much evidence of liaison between these, and the map-engraver:

> The shepherds only are conversant in the traditional annals of the mountains, and with all the secrets of the mysterious reign of chaos and old night; and they only, can give proper information concerning them; for others who live almost within the shadow of these mountains, are often ignorant of their names.

Thus speaks Thomas Gray, apropos of Styhead Pass. But in actual fact the older route of this track is clearly shown as a bridle-path on Hodskinson and Donald's map published in 1774, only four years after Gray's tour, on a scale of one inch to the mile, and on account of mining activity and the relative badness of more roundabout routes, must have been at that date a fairly well-used commercial artery.†

What was, after all, the state of civilisation and knowledge at this period? When one contrasts such productions, on the one hand, as Moll's (1724), which is on poor paper, not specially well engraved, empirically compiled, uninformed by any fresh scientific conception or by artistic conscien-

---

* As a matter of fact there was a fair on the summit of High Street (2700 feet) every year on August 10th.

† Sea-charts were in a similar state. In Captain Greenvile Collins' preface to the first edition (1694) of the sea surveys which he had been commissioned to make by Charles II, he diffidently disdains the intention of recommending to knowledgeable master mariners the bookish practice of relying on charts, but naively suggests that they might be useful in case on a long voyage the master and mates who best knew the coast had happened to die at sea. And indeed, when one looks at Collins' maps, one can only feel glad that the sailors *did* prefer to rely on their own sturdy practical sense.

tiousness, with the seventeenth-century atlases, with their gorgeous vellum bindings, their fine printing, the elegant layout of their sheets, their rich ornamentation—and even when one compares the accuracy of their contents—the intervening years seem to have borne little fruit. Even the fulsome heraldry, the outlandish costumes and (in foreign maps), the strange beasts (often observed with surprising accuracy) in the earlier maps testify to their makers' imaginative and broad conception of their department of knowledge. A similar comparison might be made of the states of many another art in the spacious days of the late Stuarts and the homelier ones of the first Georges. The favourite old maps of Saxton, Speed, and Blaeu were respectively reprinted, with little alteration, by Lea (1680), Overton (1713) and Rocque.

Although the betterment of maps may seem a little slow, they were, no doubt, in the early part of the eighteenth century, coming into the hands of many more people than the fine maps of the seventeenth century which had owed their existence to scientific zeal and royal encouragement, and were part of the necessary furniture of every great nobleman's library. The maps of the mid-century try to make up by the garrulity of their marginal notes for their deficiency in accurate surveying. 'Moll's little erroneous trifles, built upon copy, took very well.' The art of dis- seminating commercially suitably watered-down informa- tion (of journalism, in fact) was well understood by this time. An increasing public was keen to be instructed upon a large variety of subjects, among which topography was one of the most popular.

In 1746 the *Gentleman's Magazine* at its own expense promoted a survey of the coast of Cumberland, a description by the surveyor being published in 1748. 'I was made extremely sensible of the want of correct maps in the course of my survey.' Some of the errors of former maps were set down to the magnetic variation having been habitually ignored by earlier surveyors and by shipmasters. The variation, which had been nil in 1666, had increased steadily until in 1715 it was 14°, and in 1746, 17° 30″. The single chart of the Irish Sea in Greenvile Collins' *Coasting Pilot* (1756 edition) is very primitive; one would say the product of rough empiricism and not of any survey, as are some others in the same volume. But within two decades, the Cumberland coastline assumes its modern shape on maps, in common with all the remaining parts of the British coastline.

Uninspiring as it may have been, the early part of the eighteenth century was nevertheless a time of busy activity. The popularisation of common information was proceeding rapidly. Other articles in the *Gentleman's Magazine* testify to this. An account of a journey by Derbyshire to Windermere appeared in 1748, the editor remarking: 'The surveys and descriptions of several parts, which we have inserted at various times, have been received with a peculiar approbation, and a continuance of so agreeable an entertainment often requested. Could we procure more such, we should readily insert them.'

In 1747 there had appeared *A Journey to Caudebec [Caldbeck] Fells*. This seems to be from the same hand as the Tour to Borrowdale:

One curiosity is apt to excite another; after visiting Cross Fells my inclination had led me to examine those of Caudebec . . . distinguished by insuperable precipices and towering peaks, and exhibiting landscapes of a quite different and more romantic air than any part of the general ridge [this probably means the Pennines] and of nearer affinity to the Switzerland Alps.

There is a rough, semi-pictorial sketch map of the Skiddaw group of hills, with many hills named. In considering the occasional extravagant expressions about scenery, we should bear in mind the public appetite about this time for rich mixed journalistic feeding. It surprises one less to find mountains loaded with such adjectives as 'horrid' and 'stupendous' in such publications, when the descriptions are sandwiched between news items describing the 'horrid barbarities of the smugglers' in Sussex, lists of people con-

PART OF JEFFERYS WESTMORELAND, 1770

Scale: 1 inch = 1 mile

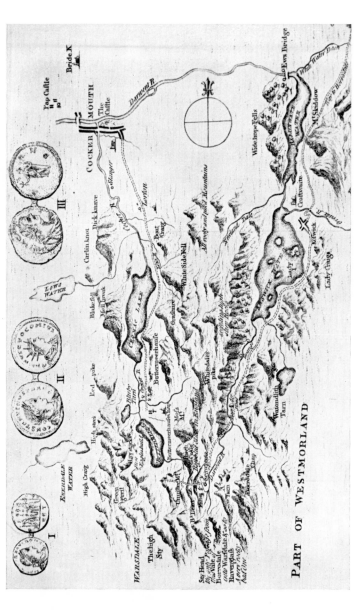

THE BLACK-LEAD MINES IN CUMBERLAND

from *Gentleman's Magazine*, 1751

demned to hang in chains, notices of monstrous calves born with five legs, and advertisements of astonishing quack remedies for complaints which themselves seem not only horrid but hardly credible.

The natives sometimes seem to have been willing to play up: 'Here I found villages in the narrow bottoms, that feel no more benefit from the solar rays, for about two months about the winter solstice, than the old Cimmerians, or the Laplanders.' Near Bowscale Tarn, says the Caldbeck visitor, the sun was not seen for four months, 'several of the most credible inhabitants affirming that they frequently see the stars in the tarn at midday'.

The article of June 1751 on the visit to Borrowdale was illustrated by a small sketch map, stated to be 'the only one ever drawn', showing the country between Cockermouth and Honister Hause. On this, the road from Cockermouth directly is shown extending no further than Buttermere, but by way of Keswick and the east side of Derwentwater a track is shown to the top of Honister Hause. No doubt the slates, which are mentioned as being quarried about Honister, were mostly conveyed by the well-known high-level route known as 'Moses Sledgate' down into Wasdale for the shipment by sea from Ravenglass. In the same article, botanical notes begin to appear: 'The plants of Skiddaw are: Myrtle berries, generally called blackberries, the vitis idaea of Dioscorides, mossberries, great variety of mosses, and among others the muscus squamosus pulcher digitatus of Tournefort.'

Mountains and other areas of low economic value, such as coastal dunes and saltings and the swampy borders of lakes, are still for a long while afterwards the step-children of the map-maker. Whilst in the seventeenth century a conventional sign or group of such signs was used to indicate, in the most general way, the approximate position of mountain passes and hilly areas, conspicuous peaks and celebrated knolls all alike, by the middle of the eighteenth century there is some attempt to define, by sketching, the

c

lower escarpments or limits of mountain masses, but the
result of this is that the main ridges themselves are even less
well shown than before.

On Bowles' and Sayers' map of 1760 the fells between
Buttermere and Cockley Beck make their first bow, jointly,
as 'Darwent Fells Mountains' but no others than our old
friends 'Skiddaw Hill' and 'Helvillon Hill' appear indivi-
dually. The most remarkable feature of this map, followed
by some others, is a road running nearly straight from Whitehaven by 'Ennerdale' (some miles below the much shrunken
'Broadwater') to Wasdale Chapel and thence straight again
to Hawkshead, passing some way north of the Three Shire
Stone. I am of opinion that this route is not intended for the
track by Burnmoor to Eskdale and thence over Hardknott,
but for that by Styhead and Esk Hause to Langdale (never,
of course, possible for vehicles) and onwards by Blea Tarn
and Tarn Hows to Hawkshead. Gray's mention of a route
to Hawkshead branching off the Styhead Pass gives some
support to this.

On the same map, it will also be noticed that the main
Carlisle road from the South does not, between Carnforth
and Kendal, follow the course either of the modern road by
Milnthorpe or of that by Crooklands. Two or three miles
north of Burton the route departed from the latter road and
proceeded by Sallatbrow and Natland. This is apparently
also the route intended to be shown in Ogilby's road book
of 1675.

The only other Lakeland road shown by Ogilby and the
other eighteenth-century Road Books is that from Kendal by
Keswick to Cockermouth (for Carlisle) which Ogilby said
was 'as bad as any in England, being very hilly, stony and
moorish'. However, West's *Guide* in 1778 was actually able
to claim the quality of the roads as an inducement in itself
to visit the country, as he says they had been much improved
since Gray's tour, and even Pennant's tour of 1772. Local
gentlemen, he says, had set a precedent by opening carriage
roads for visitors at private expense, and the public roads

were properly attended to. An example is Lord Lewis
Gordon, who built one of the roads along the west side of
Derwentwater. In the seventeen-sixties the principal roads
of Westmorland became turnpikes.

In 1800 Housman could say that 'perhaps no county in
the kingdom can boast of better roads than those of Westmorland'. Wrynose and Hardknott passes then constituted 'an
uneasy but passable road'; at Kirkstone 'the surface is very
rugged until it reaches the vale', after which it was good to
Penrith, and the whole road by Dunmail Raise was very
good.

The last decades of the century saw a complete trans-
formation in mapping. In 1759 the Society of Arts, recognising the general inaccuracy of the maps of the time, offered
a bonus of £100 for a new map, at one inch to the mile,
based on actual survey, of each county in England. This
resulted in the production of maps of an altogether superior
type: of Westmorland (and of Yorkshire) by Thomas
Jeffreys in 1770 and of Cumberland by Messrs. Hodskinson
and Donald in 1774. Lancashire, by Yates, did not appear
complete until 1786. On these maps, for the first time not
merely a very few main roads but all the roads are shown,
and with accuracy comparable to that of a modern map on
the same scale. Most of the farms are named, and indeed
show up very clearly, freed from the encumbering detail of
modern developments.

With these fine maps, it is for the first time a shorter story
to say where they are wrong than where they succeed. Only
in respect of certain kinds of natural features are they still
rather sketchy. The outlines of the lakes, and, in some cases,
of the sea-coast, are imperfect in detail, and it has not
occurred to anyone to be interested in the true shape of a
mountain as shown by contours or even by the careful hill-
shading of the mid-nineteenth century.

Hill names now appear in large numbers; their position
and relative importance begins to fall into place, and only
the shape is unreliable. It is surprising, however, that the

name of Gable should be missing, when such hills as Seat-allan, Pillar, Steeple, Haycock, and High Stile are named; although Scafell Pike is not differentiated from Scafell proper.

A certain amount of additional detail can be gleaned from some more local surveys, or sketch maps, often produced for tourists, by guides and others, although most of these cannot seriously be regarded as competitors with the county maps, as regards quality. One of the most elaborately produced of these was the work of one James Clarke, Land Surveyor, of Penrith, who in 1787 published *A Survey of the Lakes of Cumberland, Westmoreland and Lancashire.* His maps do not cover the whole of the district by any means, but only (in separate plates) the borders of Windermere, Derwentwater, Bassenthwaite, Ullswater and the roads from Keswick to Penrith and to Windermere, with the lands adjoining (this including also Grasmere, Rydal, and Thirlmere), all on a scale large enough to show clearly the position and even the shape of buildings and the boundaries of fields. Clarke explains: 'The business of the following plans is to conduct the stranger to those places which furnish the views and landscapes of different kinds in the neighbourhood of the Lakes, and which the taste of the times has been so pleased with.' Although one or two accounts of mountain ascents are contained in his book, Clarke says nothing about conducting the stranger to the fell-tops. In 1787, the stranger seldom thought of visiting these. On his maps, Clarke barely recognises their existence, by the words which appear as a sort of headline along the top of his map of the road from Keswick to Ambleside: 'From here are very high mountains to Ambleside.' Although William Green, Christopher North, and others knew many of the mountains pretty well by about 1820, Jonathan Otley was the first guide-book writer to make a real attempt to ascertain their heights and to include accurate directions in his *Guide.*

From the time of the county maps of Jeffreys, Hodskinson and Yates, the map-maker may be said to have mastered his material, and although later maps such as Greenwood's may be handsome in themselves, or may record a bygone countryside, their cold correctitude hardly compensates in interest for the wayward charm of the older maps. At last, in 1860, the Ordnance Survey published its maps of Cumberland, the last county in their series, which had been begun in 1801.

CHAPTER IV

EXCURSION INTO FANTASY

RELIEVED from old terrors and discomforts, people in the more comfortable walks of life could afford sensibility, not to say eccentricity, and enjoy feeling their flesh creep slightly.

The rising fashion which had already begun before the mid-century, under the patronage of coteries in high life such as that of Horace Walpole, rapidly filtered downwards among those who aspired to taste. The rococo style of ornament, current in France a few years earlier, now from about 1740 onwards came into vogue in England, that is to say in sophisticated circles, followed by the outlandish and the sham 'Gothick'. Waterfalls gushed from the title pages of books, and even (in carving) from mirror frames and cabinets, whilst pagoda-roofs, ruined abbeys and blasted trees became universal artistic properties. In regard to actual mountains, Horace Walpole himself seems rather to have shared the older point of view and, on his journey to Italy in 1739, found the rocks of the Mont Cenis merely 'uncouth' and scarcely even pleasurably horrifying. His taste in romanticism bore as little truthful relation to nature as it did to the mediaeval or Chinese history or architecture which were its material. The robust enjoyment by the upper-class English party of the glaciers of Chamonix did not come until 1747. For such dilettanti as Walpole, the force of untamed nature was only grand or noble when felt at a distance.

In the laying out of parks and gardens, the same sort of sensational effect was frequently aimed at. Dr. Samuel Johnson, on his tour to Wales in 1772, wrote of 'the striking scenes' and 'terrific grandeur' of Hawkestone Park in Staffordshire, of the 'awfulness of its shadow', the 'horrors of its precipices', of 'inaccessible altitude' and 'horrible profundity'. In the very year before this, Johnson had accomplished the really arduous voyage to the Hebrides, but never thought it necessary to speak in the least like this of the Cuillin mountains, an omission which has surprised many. Perhaps the Skye weather never let him see them. But in any case he is only echoing a conventional tone of exaggerated sensibility, by way of compliment to a work of art in the 'sublime' style of landscape gardening. Partly because of his physical defects, partly by disposition and training, he really cared nothing either way: literature and human behaviour were his whole life, and he never really appreciated either pictures, gardens, scenery, music, or anything else of that sort, at first-hand. Boswell, who liked flirting with all kinds of ideas, may have been testing Johnson's reactions to the cant phrases of the new romantic fashion when he invited the Sage's admiration for 'yonder immense mountain' in Glen Shiel. 'No sir,' said Johnson, 'it is merely a considerable protuberance.'

Too much can easily be made of our forefathers' alleged dread of, and their horrified fascination by, the wilder aspects of nature. In the days when warfare raged, the world over, in the interests of the nascent British Empire, toilsome journeys were all in the day's work. The poor Lichfield youth who had walked up to London, and had slept out hungry nights in the London squares, saw little romance in privation. In his struggling days, the tastes of Horace Walpole's circle were not for him.

The more sensational triumphs in this style were, of course, for the privileged few. The preferences of less advanced people were, typically, for a landscape in which different elements, in proper proportions, set each other off. James Boswell, for once in his judicious rather than in his more elevated mood, briefly notes one such for us: 'We saw before us a beautiful bay, well defended by a rocky coast; a good family mansion, a fine verdure about it, with a considerable number of trees, and beyond it hills and mountains in gradation of wildness.' This is not really so much different from Camden's admiring description of Cumberland 200 years before.

In the recently-published *Journals*, a new Boswell is revealed to us, of depths hitherto hardly suspected. Whatever he may have admitted to his mentor, Boswell was, or had it in him to become, a devotee of romantic scenery. Neither was this, as so often, one of those stylish characters which he, sometimes more and sometimes less successfully, tried to make his own, but a cry from that excessive original sensibility of his which he constantly feared, and tried to control. On first leaving Edinburgh for London, had he not gone alone, to take, with deliberate ceremony, in which deep feeling and mawkishness seem equally blended, his farewell of Arthur's Seat?—'on which I have so often strayed in my days of youth, and felt the raptures of a soul filled with the magnificence of God and his creation'. Ought we indeed to recognise him as the founder and patron of our British mountain cult, who beneath an unimpressive exterior concealed as romantic a love of at least one mountain as any suburban hiker? During his life, he found occasion to visit a fair amount of what we now know as picturesque scenery, in Switzerland, Corsica, and the Hebrides. It was, it is true, Corsican or Highland chieftains whom he was stalking, not merely the maquis or the moorland among which they lived, but the habitat of Paoli or Mcghillichalum was an essential part of the portrait. Though he was neither physically strenuous nor bold, he cannot have been averse to incurring the amount of fatigue the quest of the picturesque demanded. His namby-pambyness at the age of 22 may have been outgrown ten years later. To visit the Hebrides for any reason at all was no mean effort—too great an effort almost for anyone who did not enjoy that sort of thing for itself. There are plenty of indications in his journals of the powerful influence of place on his spirits, nor was the sensibility denied him to have become a leader in the appreciative description of scenery. But, in the impressionable years of his earliest manhood, his mind and his ambitions were otherwise engaged. As his journals reveal—those journals which show us so different a Boswell from the Dr. Samuel Johnson's biographer—he was deeply concerned to hold in check and conceal from the outer world the imaginative side of his nature. This was present in excess, dangerously perhaps by any standard, and especially by the standards of his time and social milieu. His potential growth-points were protean in their variety, but in the background was the inhibitory figure of Lord Auchinleck. Like an ownerless puppy, James was ready to lick any hand which smelled like that of a potential Master. Johnson and the Duchess of Northumberland, Voltaire and Rousseau, the Prince of Hesse and Frederick the Great—how various they were! If, in 1762, it had been fashionable to write in the style and with the interests of the authors who gave us eyes to see the Lake District, we might have had at least a secondary masterpiece from Boswell in that genre. Had he been born twenty years later, it would probably have been to Wordsworth and Coleridge that he would have turned, as did John Wilson from Edinburgh, and de Quincey, an even queerer fish than Boswell.

It is not altogether idly that I have indulged this fancy. Although it was Johnson who extended the hand, it was Rousseau above all who was the object of Boswell's pilgrimage as a young man, and it is to Rousseau that we owe a powerful strain in the ancestry of our feeling for natural scenery and of the tone in which for a time it was predominantly expressed. Two things Boswell needed: a formal framework for the resolution of his religious doubts, and a set of objective interests as a discipline. Johnson and Johnson's circle gave him these, but does his after-history indicate that they did so in the manner most completely satisfying his requirements? He would not have been the first or last to turn, in agonising spiritual struggle, to a refuge in the contemplation of nature and eventually to have been becalmed in the humdrum round of country life. Surely he can claim, more than most people, to have been born out of time. His sheer cleverness would have probably ensured him a place as a not inconsiderable Lake Poet, although certainly the secondary associations of the Lake School of Poets in after times might have been rather different as a result.

CHAPTER V

A FEARFUL JOY

While some on earnest business bent
Their murm'ring labours ply
'Gainst graver hours, that bring constraint
To sweeten liberty,
Some bold adventurers disdain
The limits of their little reign
And unknown regions dare descry:
Still as they run they look behind
They hear a voice in every wind
And snatch a fearful joy.

from *Ode on a Distant Prospect of Eton College*
by THOMAS GRAY

THERE IS, EVEN TO-DAY, a very large section of people
to whom mountains make no appeal. Considerable
physical, nervous, visual and mental readjustment is
necessary before many people brought up in really flat
countrysides can be fully at ease among mountains. Some
flatlanders are never able to get over the claustrophobic
aversion from a valley, or the corresponding dread of
heights. Probably their point of view is now as much
suppressed by convention as the opposite view used to be.
They are entitled to sympathy, and even respect. But for
people affected by such disabilities, mountain scenery has
often a dramatic force, or romantic appeal, in inverse proportion to their familiarity with it. It was from Cambridge
that Thomas Gray set out in 1769 on his now famous tour
of the Lakes. Born and brought up in the Home Counties,
he had, in 1737, in his second year at the university, and
while living at Burnham in Buckinghamshire, given, in a
letter to Horace Walpole, the earliest indication of his taste
for romantic scenery:

I have, at the distance of half a mile, through a green lane, a forest
(the vulgar call it a common) all my own, at least as good as so, for I

spy no human thing in it but myself. It is a little chaos of mountains and precipices: mountains, it is true, that do not ascend much above the clouds, nor are the declivities quite so amazing as Dover cliff: but just such hills as people who love their necks as well as I do may venture to climb, and craggs that give the eye as much pleasure as if they were dangerous: Both vale and hill are covered with the most venerable beeches . . . at the foot of one of these squats ME, and there grow to be a trunk for a whole morning.

Two years later, he made the Grand Tour to Italy in Walpole's company, and it was then that he found the Alpine scenery 'pregnant with religion and poetry'. Gray did not see the mountains again after this, for 25 years. A somewhat timid and slightly eccentric recluse, and not wealthy, he lived the quiet life of a college fellow at Cambridge. Perhaps, like Housman, who when he wrote his *Shropshire Lad* had never seen Shropshire, Gray found that his imaginative life flourished best in a sedentary posture.

In 1765 he made a journey to Scotland, the occasion of which was to enjoy the hospitality of Glamis Castle, which lies in the wide strath of Forfarshire. One excursion only he made from this house in the direction of the Highlands: to Blair Athole. He noticed Schiehallion and Ben-y-Gloe on the way. It was from the time of this Perthshire journey that the quest of scenery became a positive aim for Gray.

I am returned from Scotland charmed with my expedition; it is of the Highlands I speak; the lowlands are worth seeing once, but the mountains are ecstatic. None but those monstrous creatures of God know how to join so much beauty with so much horror. A fig for your poets, painters, gardeners, clergymen, that have not been among them; their imagination can be made up of nothing but bowling-greens, flowering-shrubs, horse-ponds, Fleet ditches, shell grottoes, and Chinese rails.

His health also benefited, and no doubt he wished he had had the wit many years earlier to exploit this delightful remedy for his constitutional low-spiritedness and inactivity. Or perhaps gadding off to the more barbarous fringes of the world may have seemed no fitting enterprise for a man, a learned man at that, of settled position, but were only to be undertaken by one who need no longer care about the world's opinion. So in 1769 he made his tour to the Lakes, and in the following year he died.

Gray was not of course the first to conceive the idea of a tour for the enjoyment of Lake District scenery, even if he turned out to be the most exquisite observer who had visited it up to that time. He had in him nothing of the sturdy pioneer traveller like Pennant, who at this time was systematically pressing his investigations to the remotest parts of the Scottish Highlands. However much he was attracted by the literary romance of the Gothic past, the distant, and the savage, a good deal of example from others must have been needed before he was persuaded of the possibility of seeking such experience in his own person. He had very probably read Dr. John Brown's letter* on the scenery of Keswick, addressed to Lord Lyttelton, who also was one of Horace Walpole's circle. Ducal landowners were beginning to improve the amenities of their northern domains by placing on the lakes barges, which in their absence were generally available for the use of travellers of respectable appearance who had gift of angling tactfully for favours.

The artists had already been working the Lake District: William Bellers in 1752 and Thomas Smith of Derby in 1761. The latter's prints Gray had seen, but it may have been on his tour—and not previously. There must already have been a substantial purchasing public for these engravings, which were of as high a class as any that were produced later. Certain excursions and sights seem to have been expected of the visitor even in Gray's time.

The credit, not indeed for beginning the movement towards appreciation of scenery in the romantic spirit, but for being the first, so far as the Lake District is concerned, to provide a published record of an expedition made in that

---

* I have not been able to find at what date this letter was written. West's *Guide* says it was printed at Newcastle in 1767—after Brown's death, which took place in 1758.

spirit, belongs perhaps to the author of an article in the
Gentleman's Magazine of 1751. He tells of a journey in August
1749 to see the plumbago or 'wad' mines at Seathwaite in
Borrowdale. This sort of subject was just the kind, thoroughly
practical yet with its romantic side, to interest the Age of
Robinson Crusoe. The party hailed from Wigton, and it is
therefore possible that the writer was either Dr. John Brown
himself, whose father was Rector at Cockermouth, not far
away, or someone of his acquaintance. His impressions on
Honister Crag were sensational in the extreme ('We turned
from this fearful prospect afraid even of ourselves') but in
the course of the same article he mentions that he had on
another occasion ascended Skiddaw. Of the view from the
top of the latter, he says: 'The craggy precipices' (of 'neighbouring mountains') 'have the appearance of huge fragments
of rock, irregularly heaped on one another, but in the
prospect round, nature has lavished such variety of beauty
as can scarce be believed upon report, or imagined by the
most luxuriant fancy.'

This same Brown it was who was author of an influential
book: *An Estimate of the Manners of the Times* published in
1757. Since the Restoration, the social attractions of town
life had markedly come to prevail over those of country life.
'Foxhunter' had long been a byword for provincial brutality
and philistinism. Brown, on the other hand, laments the
decay of horse riding among the nobility. Army officers 'in
the capital are occupied in dress, cards, and tea, and in
country towns divide their time between milliners' shops and
taverns'. He considered it a further sign of the degeneracy
of the age that, despite Hogarth's example and advocacy,
naturalistic art had been banished by the fantastic and
grotesque, represented in the extreme by the rococo and the
Chinese tastes.

Gray's claim, or rather the claim that others have made
for him, to be the leader of a new movement towards the
romantic appreciation of scenery needs much qualification.
His verse, which in his own lifetime was the published part

of his writings, is thoroughly classical in its visual images as in its language. The *Journal* of his tour was written in the form of a letter to a friend, and was not printed until 1775, when it appeared in Mason's *Life*. Certainly his visit was a landmark, as that of a man of recognised taste and literary esteem, and his opinions no doubt easily gained currency enough by the private circulation of the manuscript. One may distinguish the pleasure which he derived from picturesque scenery, hardly less a novelty to him than the notion of it was to contemporary opinion, from the pleasure in simple nature, which he had always enjoyed in a high degree, and which could be no novelty or exclusive possession at all, irrespective of aesthetic theory. Gray had no particular wish to make converts to any theory, either philosophical or aesthetic. He did not, like a dogmatic sentimentalist, try to attribute virtue to everything connected with that which gave him pleasure—to do so would have been to deny his own gift of delicate receptivity.

He had never any wish to come to terms with physical difficulties; certainly not to spoil the pleasures of imagination by ill-placed laboriousness. Of Rydal Head he remarks: 'As for going up it, one might as well go up Skiddaw.' But he gave his critics opportunity to overrate his personal timorousness by the manner in which he wrote up the sensational aspect of parts of his journeys. It is needless to multiply instances, but one may well doubt, for example, whether he really believed that Lodore Crags were likely to fall on his head, for all that he says so, or even whether he really expected his correspondent to think that he did. It would hardly be more unfair, on the evidence of his poetical works, to accuse him of believing in fairies, or in the classical pantheon.

The following verses are said to have been found among
the literary remains of a certain poet.

ODE

on a Favourite Cat, Graymalkin Tom,
Which was not drowned in a bowl of goldfish

As on a rustic valley's side
Where fancy's gayest art had dyed
The simplest flowers that blow
Demurest of the tabby kind
The pensive T****s G**y reclined;
Gazed on the lake below.

The hapless swain with wonder saw,
With many an ardent wish—
Twitched first his whisker, then his claw—
It is no Nereid that thou saw!
Be cautious-bold! With-hold thy paw!
What glisters, is but fish.

DERWENT WATER

Chatelin's engraving, 1774, after William Bellers

PART OF DONALD'S CUMBERLAND, 1774

Scale: 1 inch = 1 mile

CHAPTER VI

ET EGO IN ARCADIA VIXI

There is a boat on
The lake to float on
And lots of beauties
Which I can't entwine
But were I a preacher
Or a classic teacher
In every feature
I'd make 'em shine.

from *The Groves of Blarney* (about 1790)

JUST TOO LATE to have been of service as an outlet to
the young Boswell, there came into vogue for a brief
decade or two a style of warm and uninhibited expression
—of indulgence of feeling—which would have suited him
well enough. Literature might not have benefited, on balance,
but Boswell might have. On the parallel plane of artistic
symbolism one may trace its currency by the veiled and
shrouded female figure, weeping over the urn, elegant on the
oval-panelled pedestal, a willow tree perhaps overhanging
the whole. I mean the climate in which subsisted elements as
various as the eccentric idealism of Thomas Day, the panti-
socracy of the young Coleridge and Southey, the noble
liberalism of Charles Fox, and the affectations Robert Burns
found in Edinburgh. The intimacies which Gray or Walpole
had reserved for semi-private letters were now current coin
of the country churchyard or market-place. Churchyard?
Why, because the style, so congenial for the purpose of
elegies, is kept in our memory, as it is nowadays, mainly by
enduring marble. The subject of death was just what was
required for the strong dramatic themes the style called for,
and was a popular choice. In the appreciation of our Lakeland scenery its representative was William Hutchinson.

D

Over-lush as it tended to be, it did not endure long enough
to become stale, and we can mourn it as something cut off
untimely, by the actualities of the Revolution in France and
the Industrial Revolution, the fear of Jacobinism at home,
and the return of war.

Not that this elegiac style was always reserved for dealing
with gloomy subjects. It has perhaps more claim than any
other to be regarded as the classic one for the appreciative
description of British scenery, with which it was contemporary. That scenery (the *Oxford English Dictionary* dates
the word 'scenery' itself from 1784) was being noted, com-
mented upon, recognised, and regularised not only in the
Lake District alone but in half a dozen areas of Britain at
almost the same time. Preserved for us in probably uninten-
tional parody, the verses from County Cork, from which I
have already quoted at the head of the chapter, display in
their earliest freshness many of the very same features that
struck the first sentimental observers of the district of the
Lakes. There, too, do we hear about such things as a cave
where no daylight enters; where cats and badgers are forever
bred; which, mossed by nature, makes it completer than a
downy bed. 'Tis there the lake is, well stored with fishes, and
comely eels in the verdant mud; beside the leeches, and
groves of beeches standing in order to guard the flood.

Those who care for virtuosity in description will enjoy
William Hutchinson's *Excursion to the Lakes in Westmoreland
and Cumberland in the years 1773 and 1774* which was published
in 1776. By profession he was an attorney at Barnard Castle.
His tour was undertaken largely for archaeological purposes,
but he was everywhere on the look-out for scenic effects, and
mixes up boating, and listening to echoes, with Roman
antiquities in the most naïve way. Rhetorical 'sensibility' in
literary treatment of life's affairs generally, was at this time
approaching its high-water mark, and an emotional level is
consistently maintained throughout the book, except where
strictly archaeological matter is under discussion, when he
at once becomes thoroughly business-like.

In order to examine this fortress (Brough Castle) with greater attention, I revisited it the succeeding year.—When I attempt to give a reason
for my second visit to the Lakes, and beating the same road again, my
eyes swim with tears, and my heartrending sorrow is renewed to me in
all its energy, for the inestimable loss I have sustained since my first
excursion, in my fellow-traveller, my draughtsman, my friend, my
second half, my *Brother*; his virtues were too excellent to be detained
from heaven: he departed in the flower of youth, amidst all the fire of
genius, in the twentythird year of his age—see Plate IV.

Hutchinson conjures up what will be to many an ideal
picture of the eighteenth-century Man of Feeling among the
mountains. The ugly utilitarian philistinism of the world of
Defoe and Hogarth, the Johnsonian apogee of common-
sense, are things of the past. It is time to explore, in a more
genial frame of mind, if perhaps with a little too much
abandonment, the less well charted aspects of nature and of
sensibility.

He can admire the spectacle of the stag-hunt on the
Martindale fells, and equally confess his sympathy with the
hunted beast. All the charms of English scenery and historical topography unspoilt by the crowd await discovery,
at the distance only of a week or two's pleasant travel. The
generation of Walpole and of Gray indeed began the Exodus,
but their pride, their prejudices, their fear of ridicule, barred
them out of Canaan. In his letters Gray indeed has flashes of
poetic feeling which he did not suppress any more than he
attempted to explain them. Hutchinson can hardly be compared with Gray as an artificer in words. But Hutchinson
has the advantage of not having to keep up the reputation
of a university wit. In latter times, such luscious sentiment
as his would have been thought to go badly in harness with
his archaeological interests, but he is able to throw himself
equally into both. All this outpouring of soulfulness, it is
not perhaps quite what one would think had survival value
for a country lawyer? Rather, I should think the nimble-
wittedness which allowed him to strike so successfully the
fashionable note of the decade—even apart from the power
to lay it aside 'at the drop of a hat'—makes it needless for

us to be anxious about his professional fortunes. A man to make juries weep, but at the same time with the soundest grasp of essential documents and Bills of Costs! Of one like him, who has kissed the Blarney Stone, we may hope that

> 'tis he may clamber
> to a lady's chamber
> or become a member
> of sweet parliament.

Considered impersonally, as a writer, his merit is his genuine perceptiveness, which is not altogether disguised by either his fluency, his over-heightened tone, or, for us nowadays, his too-allusive vocabulary. As he carefully notes such things as the transparency of water, the awesomeness of echoes, the imaginative stimulus of sound, colour, space, he is a child making his first steps in the delightful grammar of scenery. He is far indeed from the plain men of Defoe's time, who had frankly found mountains 'hideous' and 'frightful'.

We shall not be altogether surprised to find that Hutchinson, on Ullswater, was able to secure the use of the Duke of Portland's barge.

The vessel was provided with six brass cannon mounted on swivels;—on discharging one of these pieces, the report was echoed from the opposite rocks, where by reverberation it seems to roll from cliff to cliff and return through every cave and valley; till the decreasing tumult gradually died away on the ear. . . .

At intervals we were relieved from this entertainment, which consisted of a kind of wondrous tumult and grandeur of confusion, by the music of two French horns, whose harmony was repeated from every recess which echo haunted on the borders of the Lake; here the breathings of the organ were imitated, there the bassoon with clarinets;—in this place from the harsher sounding cliffs, the cornet;—in that from the wooded creek, amongst the caverns and the trilling waterfalls, we heard the soft-toned lute accompanied with the languishing strains of enamoured nymphs; whilst in the copse and grove was still retained the music of the horns. All this vast theatre was possessed by innumerable aerial beings, who breathed celestial harmony.

Finally, by a general discharge of the guns

the sounds were reverberated from side to side, so as to give the semblance of that confusion and horrid uproar, which the falling of these stupendous rocks would occasion, if by some internal combustion they were rent to pieces, and hurled into the lake.

The use of guns and musical effects generally for the sake of their echoes, as well as to supply an adjunct to scenery, remained in favour for more than half a century after this time. In due course, most of the better Lakeland hotels which happened to be favourably situated, such as Lowwood, were equipped with cannon.

The association of music with water parties was no new thing. Horace Walpole mentions an occasion on which the Prince of Wales had two boat-loads of musicians on the Thames. This sort of thing was, of course, a rich man's pastime. But the average Cumberland dale could scarcely be relied on to produce, as, when, and where fancy might call for it, even a competent hornplayer—hence the regrets of traveller after traveller. William Green thought that 'plaintive solos on the clarionet or flute would have a fine effect among such rocks'; and, despite his own disapproval of turning nature into a peep-show, even Wordsworth unbent: 'What a grand effect the music of the bugle-horn would have among these mountains!' Here and there, in places as different as Ireland and Switzerland, one can still enjoy one's scenery to the accompaniment of the old simple and romantic type of musical effects, but it is apparently to the increased sophistication of music itself that the practice has become a victim. The more dramatic and insistent style of the nineteenth-century composers—the Schumanns, the Liszts, the Wagners—was less grateful to the genius of the enamoured nymphs and other aerial beings than that of Handel and Mozart. In bringing into the music itself the unrest of winds and waves, the agony of the benighted wanderer and the like, they made of the music no longer a tinted viewing-glass but a complete dramatic spectacle, fit to engross all one's attention. Or, as some have felt with such poems as Housman's *Shropshire Lad*, the highly-worked intensity and subjectivity will not stand contact with the actualities of the outdoor world by which they are supposed to be inspired.

But to return to Hutchinson, now arrived at the head of Ullswater:

Now all around us being one scene of mountains, which hemmed us in, arising with awful and precipitate fronts;—here the white cliffs raised their pointed heads, there the shaken and rifted rocks were split and cavated into vast shelves, chasms, and dreary cells, which yawned upon the shadowed lake; whilst other steeps less rugged were decked with shrubs . . . their summits being embrowned with sun-parched moss and scanty herbage . . . the scene was nobly awful.

Here is another of his rather Sitwellian word-pictures:

Where the lake narrows, and runs up in a creak towards Borodale, the rocks looked tremendous, almost shutting us in from the face of heaven; the cliffs were struck with scanty gleams of light, which gained their passage through the interstices of the hills, or chasms in the rocks, and served only to discover their horrible overhanging fronts; their mighty caverns, where the water struck by our oars made a hollow sound; their deformed and frowning brows, the hanging shrubs with which they were bearded, their sparkling waterfalls that trilled from shelf to shelf, the whole half seen and half concealed, leaving imagination at large to magnify the images of their grandeur and horrible magnificence.

So far, Hutchinson's tour closely followed Gray's as far as the entrance of Borrowdale, and as far up Ullswater as Watermillock, with the addition of an excursion by boat. But being young and active, he also undertook the ascent of Skiddaw. No difficulty was found in this, except that 'respiration seemed to be performed with a kind of asthmatic oppression'.

Whilst we remained upon the mountain . . . dense and dark vapours began to arise; and in a little time, as they advanced upon a south-west wind, concealed those heights we had viewed half an hour before clear and distinct.—Our guide was very earnest with us to quit the mountain. The circumstance was too singular to be left by people curious in their observations on natural events; we desired our guide would take care of himself, and leave us to our pleasure, but the good attendant had a due sense of our impropriety in wishing to be left there, and determined to abide by us—the clouds advanced with accelerated speed; a hollow

blast sounded amongst the hills and dells which lay below, and seemed
to fly from the approaching darkness.

We were rejoicing in this grand spectacle of nature, and thinking
ourselves fortunate in having beheld so extraordinary an event, when . . .
a violent burst of thunder, engendered in the vapour below, stunned
every sense, in horrid uproar . . . the mountain seemed to tremble . . .
our guide lay upon the earth terrified and amazed, in his ejaculations,
accusing us of presumption and impiety . . . danger made us solemn, we
had no place to fly for safety, no place to cover our heads; to descend,
was to rush into the inflammable vapour from whence our troubles
proceeded, to stay was equally hazardous. . . .

But forbear, gentle reader, on Hutchinson's behalf the
tribute of a moist eye, a fluttering heart. He has no need of
pity. He is enjoying himself to the top of his bent; and, when
the right moment comes, extricates himself easily with his
characteristic heartless adroitness: 'We descended the hill
wet and fatigued, and were happy when we regained our inn
at Keswick.' Just that.

CHAPTER VII

THE CORRECTLY PICTURESQUE

Long ere these happier days of genuine taste
Which give thy magic scenes encomium due
Through many an age, with like enchantment graced,
Thy rills kept tinkling, and thy thickets grew.—1780.

COUNTRYSIDE AND NATIVE PURSUITS had emerged at last from the limbo of an unfashion to which the Age of Reason had damned them. Gray remarked, in a tone of mild surprise, that his landlord at Kendal was 'civil and sensible', that is, a civilised, sentient fellow-being, not one whose only mode of greeting was to slap one on the back, and who would be likely to offer one nothing for breakfast but beer, oatcakes, and bacon. This sort of thing has its importance in the cult of scenery. The number of bourgeois travelling, from choice, to an appreciable distance from their homes had been growing steadily; first to suburb, like John Gilpin of London Town, then to spa, then (soon after the middle of the eighteenth century) to sea-bathing, or even, like the Wordsworths, to Lowland Scotland and the fringe of the Highlands. From about 1810, the already-existing English tourist herd was let loose in the Central Highlands by the writings of Scott.*

An eighteenth-century pleasure tour included the great houses on the route, to which the public-spirited owners were ready to permit access on a semi-private footing, to persons of genteel appearance. The traveller was accustomed to admire the façade in the style of Palladio, and the still newer landscape garden with its allusions to classical scenes,

---

* At the little church of St. John's in the Vale, near Thirlmere, is a tombstone to a young man who was drowned in 1802 at Oban 'in the Highlands of Scotland'. The quoted words are prominent in large Gothic lettering, as who should say, in the wilds of Abyssinia'.

its surprise view and the grotto where perhaps the hermit was paid to sit, as well as the gallery of marbles and paintings acquired, with greater or less degree of judgment, by the young heir on his tour in Italy. Public collections were rare, and artists and the public were therefore dependent to a great extent on such favours.

Very often, of course, His Grace was from home, and the statuary left to the admiration only of the housekeeper.

> The character of the ancient nobleman, living in splendour and hospitality among his country vassals and neighbours, nay, even that of the country gentleman, is almost extinguished. To see so many noble mansions adorned with painting and sculpture, and placed amid such glorious scenery, deserted . . . etc.

So writes a visitor making the Northern Tour the year after William Gilpin, with whom this chapter is mainly concerned. Possibly, however, these complaints of absenteeism need not be taken very seriously; they must be as old as the decay of feudalism, besides being an obvious stock subject for anyone with a taste for homily. The gentry were of course the leaders in the taste for landscape gardening and for romantic landscape.

So, their admiring remarks muffled by their hats held deferentially in front of their faces, by favour of his upper servants the visitors tiptoed round His Grace's gallery, hoping perhaps that their commendations might be overheard, in case after all he were not at Almack's. Even when they were resident, the owners felt, as Horace Walpole himself did, a need to display their treasures to someone, though they might be no more altruists than he. At the more modest houses, buried in the country, they were not sorry to see an occasional visitor. William Gilpin, on his way northwards, visited Mr. Shenstone's Leasowes, Lord Lyttleton's Hagley, and Mr. Anson's Shuckborough. William Combe, in his satirical *Doctor Syntax*, with its Rowlandson illustrations, does not overlook the convivial aspect of such tours, but as applied to Gilpin himself, Combe's suggestions were certainly quite slanderous.

By such means as these, many people were by now familiar
with the three styles of landscape painting which were
recognised: the reposeful and majestic style of Poussin, the
warm, serene, atmospheric style of Claude Lorrain, and the
sinisterly suggestive romantic style of Salvator Rosa. With
so much of the origins of their literature in the classics and
of their art in Italy, men had been apt to consider it a
profanation of their more idealistic and imaginative conceptions to apply them to the present, and had conventionally
assigned to them a habitation in the ages of antiquity and in
the landscapes of the South. Now they began to wonder if
the familiar English landscape could not be moulded into
similar artistic form.

> And did those feet in ancient time
> Walk upon England's mountains green
> And was the Holy Lamb of God
> In England's pleasant pastures seen?
> And did the Countenance divine
> Shine forth upon our clouded hills?

George III, as a young man, had 'gloried in the name of
Briton'. England turned her gaze inwards on herself, and,
as we see somewhat later from the paintings of Morland and
Wheatley, the geographical position of Arcady was considered to be no longer in the Mediterranean but nearer
home. But it was a long time before English picture buyers
were completely educated out of expecting England's landscapes to be predominantly brown, like the varnish of old
pictures to which they were accustomed.

Travel for the enjoyment of scenery had next to pass from
being a mere personal foible to the possession of rules and
principles of its own. An important part in this stage of its
exploitation was played by William Gilpin, a clergyman and
schoolmaster in Surrey, who published in 1786 his book
*Observations relative to Picturesque Beauty made on a tour to
Cumberland and Westmoreland*, made in the year 1772. His task
was to rationalise, or, as Dr. Johnson would have said, to
'moralise' the new fashion.

Gilpin came of an old family in Cumberland, where he spent his boyhood. It is reassuring to know this, since in his book he virtually says, in more than one place, that his whole acquaintance with the Lake District extended over less than a week.

We may think that Combe, who tells of his hero's exploits in eating, drinking and picaresque adventures, and often winds up a canto by describing him falling into a stream or being robbed, hardly takes advantage of the real proneness to satire of Gilpin's book and does not in fact succeed in being as amusing as his victim. To do Gilpin justice, it is impossible to miss the ultra-dry flavour of irony in a good deal that he wrote.

Gilpin was far from being a deeply original mind; and it is precisely because of this that his books enjoyed so much direct and immediate influence and went through so many editions. He did not discover the Lake District, nor originate sightseeing tours there; he came a long time after the birth of the picturesque. He merely was able to offer, at the right moment and in convenient and authoritative form, exactly the handbook that already-numerous, sheep-like, upper-middle-brows were unconsciously feeling the need of. Before this time, the man in the street (or perhaps one should say, 'the man in the post-chaise') who genuinely felt the beauty of a mountain landscape found it very hard to say why, in the absence of accepted critical principle or even vocabulary. In *Nineteen Eighty Four*, the late George Orwell showed us that none but unusually powerful minds can even entertain thoughts above the most simple level in the absence of language in which to express them. Gilpin gave the tourists their Duckspeak. Before this, their inability to express their natural feelings in the presence of noble scenery, and their consequent reluctance to acknowledge them, explains a good deal of the expressed interest of ordinary eighteenth-century travellers in archaeology or other recondite subjects. They had to pretend to travel for a definite object of some kind, just as in the nineteenth century people used to go abroad 'to drink the waters'. No doubt one could carry the example down to the present day, and wonder whether the ostensible and now-respectable desire to reach the summit-points of mountains fully accounts for the efforts put forth by professed mountaineers in their pursuit.

Gilpin now relieved these people of the trouble of grubbing among masses of dilapidated masonry (of the original design of which they had often very little correct perception) or of collecting rather dull statistics about agriculture, or lending their attention as in duty bound to improbable local anecdotes, and, like Dionysus of old, demanded nothing of his followers but a flow of facile chatter, and the light burden of a sketch-book. So it was that England, and, with a difference, Scotland, learnt to see herself anew.

In criticising a picture it was of course perfectly permissible to suggest any alteration, no matter how drastic, to produce a harmony of colour or balance of mass or other desired effect. What Gilpin set out to do was to apply the accepted art-criticism to natural scenes; and so we occasionally find him lightly suggesting the most sweeping changes: say, the removal of Helvellyn to the other side of Thirlmere, or its division into three.

Gilpin's books are the meeting place of several diverse schools of ideas, some already in decline, and some more fully developed at a later date. Some of these inconsistencies he perceived, and tried to harmonise, but others remain to astonish us. But his clearest note is that of the new respect for nature, of unwillingness to do violence to her either by formality or by inappropriate ornament.

'The author's fear is that he may be thought too severe in his strictures on scenes of art. The grand natural scene will always appear so superior to the embellished artificial one that the picturesque eye in contemplating the former will be too apt to look contemptuously on the latter.'

Nature, however, is to understand that the liberty conferred on her is only a liberty to do well. She is expected to offer a limitless succession of landscapes apt for transferring to canvas. Thus he says: 'With all this magnificence and beauty it cannot be supposed that every scene which these countries present is correctly picturesque.' The imagination of the artist is, therefore, required to correct nature's 'prentice essays. 'We deviated into a mere scene of mountains. Nature seemed to have attempted some mode of composition which she had left unfinished but it was difficult to conceive what species of landscape she meant; a valley or a wooded recess, a cultivated scene or a wild one.'

The pupil is indeed admitted to possess talent. 'We may remark . . . that the power which imagination hath over these scenes is not greater than the power which they have over the imagination . . . the wild follies of untutored genius often strike the imagination more than the most correct effusions of cultivated parts.'

It is therefore a matter of some anxiety with Gilpin how far the artist may depart from the strict portraiture of nature. In solving the problem he is hampered in several ways: first, perhaps, by a hesitation in finally renouncing the association which landscape painting before the days of photography necessarily had with mere topographical draughtsmanship. Then, interest in the natural beauty which was the main topic of his book would perhaps be jeopardised if it were not faithfully represented. A greater difficulty was ignorance of the true character of the admired scenes which, as he quite rightly, though dimly, felt, made it most likely that any alteration would be an inappropriate one. An observer with a true appreciation of the underlying rock structure and texture, or of botanical nature might be at liberty to recombine the typical elements of a scene as pictorial considerations might dictate: not so the landscape artists of the period.

Again selectivity and allusiveness are permissible where the public's familiarity with the subject-matter can be safely presumed. But, as we have said, pictures had to do a double if not a treble duty; as correct representations for those who required a souvenir of their tour, next as propaganda for a fresh source of natural beauty, and lastly as works of imaginative art.

Nature too must comport herself, not only within the bounds of pictorial composition, but also with regard to other kinds of respectability. The mediaeval framework of thought dies hard. It was perhaps not until Manet that artists, or the ordinary run of them, were content with merely visual phenomena without moral overtones. Thus Gilpin considers that 'the Lake' (generalised) whose

magnificent and marble bed . . . received originally the pellucid waters of some rushing torrent is more suitable as the subject of a picture than 'the Fen' or 'the Pool' which are in summer a seat of putrefaction; and the receptacle of all those unclean, misshapen forms of animal life which breed and batten in the impurities of stagnation.

So far even as it goes, Gilpin's respect for the integrity of nature is not an impersonal reverence for the mighty processes which made the mountains, but is really a plea for the exclusion of sentimentally discordant objects from the scenes in which his own fancy best flourishes. His book gains piquancy from the way different ideas of this kind are made to lie down side by side, without being fully reconciled.

This was the era when imitation Gothic ruins were run up, such as that on the island near Conishead Priory, and several others in Lakeland. On his island on Derwentwater, Mr. Joseph Pocklington had already run up a whole range of them, including a bogus stone circle, a make-believe church, and a sham fort. Gilpin's veritable passion for ruins is based entirely on their value for sentiment or scenery, and not, properly speaking, on any archaeological interest. When dealing with genuine ruins, he seems to forget entirely that they were ever put up for any other purpose. 'Ruins are commonly divided into two kinds, castles and abbeys.' 'The most beautiful species of architecture in which our ruins are composed is called the Gothic.' It was not the introduction of such innocent and charming erections as artificial ruins which could do violence to a landscape as nature has left it. The English Gothic he prefers to the style of foreign castles

and abbeys on the ground that a larger proportion of it lay
ruined.

He craves too for dark legends to people the romantic
scenes. Of Dunmail Raise he says: 'Nothing could suit such
a landscape better than a group of banditti. Of all the scenes
I ever saw this was the most adapted to the perpetration of
some dreadful deed. The imagination can hardly avoid
conceiving . . .' etc. etc. And of another place: 'A dreadful
story is an admirable introduction to an awful scene. It
rouses the mind and adds double terror to every precipice.'
The banditti-and-ruin craze is at worst a rather amiable and
appealing folly, hardly sillier than some more recent
varieties of sentiment suggested by mountain scenery. Such
was the love of nature in the time of the Romantic Revival,
an idyllic honeymoon which could not last forever. For the
closer and more accurate knowledge which the movement
itself very soon brought about let in the full light of day, as
it were, into the dark and misty vales of the Lakes. The
detailed and matter-of-fact style of Gilpin's own recipes for
producing picturesque effects must itself have gone far to
banish the element of the unknown and terrible in which
romantic fancies flourish. His own constant tendency
throughout (whether this is his personal characteristic or the
consequence of his opinions) is to have things both ways.

He is generally far too busy in his itinerary giving practical
directions, now to nature, now to the tourist, for the improvement and appreciation of scenery to have time to worry
like some travellers about the chances of mountains leaning
suddenly over to bury him in their debris. Even Honister
Crag, at which most authors shuddered, he contemplates
with artistic detachment; but he does not forget to wind up
the general part of his remarks on the Lake Country by a
catalogue of a few bogeys or terrors which might come in
useful as stage properties to heighten the romantic effect.
These include avalanches of snow, falls of cliffs, which
'produce one of the greatest scenes of terror which belongs
to this romantic country', the helm wind, 'violent ebullitions

of water' which 'the boatman will descry (happy that it is so) at a distance', waterspouts falling upon mountains, and 'vast bodies of water collected in the entrails of mountains' which, without any warning, force a way through their sides.

Gilpin wrote during the great epoch of landscape gardening. Capability Brown, who devised the naturalistic 'English' style, was dead, and Humphrey Repton (the first to assume the title of 'landscape gardener') reigned in his stead. The merits of different types of actual landscape were hotly debated, and the respective claims of residential convenience and of picturesque effect, 'sublimity' and 'beauty' were weighed. Uvedale Price, the wealthy dilettante, contended that the laying-out of estates for picturesque effect should be on the same principles as ruled the art of painting, whilst Repton, a far less consistent exponent of theory, drew on a wide professional experience. In the last decade of the eighteenth century the word 'picturesque' had become widely associated with exaggerated wildness, with roughness and eccentricity: as Repton said, 'the system of improvement by neglect and accident'. Price replied that neither imitation of nature herself nor of the higher arts when properly understood need invariably result in a landscape that was merely savage.

Richard Payne Knight may perhaps be called the puritan or left-wing partisan of the cult of scenery—one who placed nature, in her pristine state, above embellishment of any kind. We cannot follow at length the important and well-argued controversies between these people, but we shall return again to Knight. Although he probably never visited the Lake District, he exhibits the logical conclusions of some of Gilpin's ideas.

At this time when so much new material all over the world had been opened up to the amateurs of landscape by exploration and travel, it cannot be denied that local and personal prejudices played a certain part among the rival prophets. They could easily find arguments for their personal preferences, whatever these happened to be. Gilpin, who had

A VIEW OF WINANDERMEER   by Thomas Smith, 1761

THE FERRY, WINDERMERE

Engraving by Jukes and Sargent, 1808, after Thomas Walmsley. An imitation Gothic
church tower (in fact a 'station' for observation) is on the right,
with Belle Isle House on the left.

ENTRANCE INTO BORROWDALE

Merigol's engraving, 1792, after J. Smith

All further access is here barred to prying mortals—T. Gray

never been abroad, finds specious reasons for deciding that neither the lakes of Italy and Switzerland on the one hand, nor those of America or Norway on the other, could be truly picturesque. Knight, a Herefordshire squire, was keen for his own countryside. Here are his remarks on Lake District scenery:

> Oft have I heard the silly trav'ller boast
> The grandeur of Ontario's endless coast;
> Where, far as he could dart his wand'ring eye
> He nought but boundless water could descry.
> With equal reason, Keswick's favoured pool
> Is made the theme of every wandering fool.
> With bays and barren-ness have compassed round,
> With square enclosures there, and fallowed ground;
> Oe'r its deep waves no promontories tower,
> No lofty trees, high over-arched, imbower;
> No winding creek or solitary bay
> Midst pend-cut rocks or woods is seen to stray:
> But small prim islands, with blue fir-trees crowned,
> Spread their cold shadows regularly round;
> Whilst over all vast crumbling mountains rise
> Mean in their forms though of gigantic size.

The picture therefore that emerges for us from Gilpin's *Picturesque Tours* is that of a dilettante, a flâneur, to whom not only his fellow men and the art of architecture but the pageant of nature and the vast evidences of earth-building activity are no more than a plaything for his fanciful pedantry. Those who dislike schoolmasters as a professional type may find here agreeable confirmation of their prejudices. His books have been held partly responsible for the most idle sentiment about the value of picturesque landscape, prevailing down to the present time. The detachment of vision—escapism if you like to call it so—which sets the picturesque above the claims of humanity, has one kind of justification when practised by an artist of imagination, for his creative purposes; but much less when claimed on behalf of every blundering tourist, and its effects imposed on a countryside by the superior force, in Gilpin's day of wealth

E

and rank, nowadays of numbers. As a present-day Medical Officer of Health puts it, when speaking of the subject of housing, in his annual report:

These conditions may appear quaint and interesting to casual visitors, but they are disgusting and disheartening to those who have to live in them. Your Council is vigorously striving to bring water, sewerage, and electricity to the valleys as the first essential step towards cleaning up the district.

But this view of William Gilpin himself would not be correct. His *Picturesque Tours* were the rare and well-earned relaxations of a good man, deeply engaged in serious work. He was an enlightened schoolmaster and a devoted parish priest. At the age of eighty, he wrote a sketch of his own life, for inclusion in the records of his family. Mild, candid, moderate, and completely free from boastfulness, it achieves much dignity. Those of his published writings upon which he dwells a little with satisfaction are exclusively the ones, modest in their scope, written for the practical guidance of his pupils or his parishioners. In the fifty-page sketch, he says nothing about the influence of his picturesque writings, very widespread as this was, and all he says about their subject-matter is:

During the summer vacation, every year, at least after his circum-stances became easy, Mr. G. used to take a journey into some part of England. His great amusement, from his childhood, was drawing; a love for which he inherited from his father and grandfather. And his pleasure on these journeys was to make remarks on the face of the country in a picturesque light, and to take sketches of such scenes as most pleased him.

He had at first little view of publishing these remarks and sketches: the first two *Tours*, into the Wye Valley in 1770 and Cumberland in 1772, were not published until 1782 and 1786 respectively, and then only to raise money to build a village school for his parish of Boldre, in the New Forest, as were all the later *Tours*. In all, he raised £3000 by this means. One must say, however, that his opinions obtained much currency before he himself published them; but this was due to Mason's mention of them in his *Life* of Gray. The rascally William Combe's skit on him, as Doctor Syntax, mattered little to Gilpin, for when it appeared in 1812, he had been dead eight years.

CHAPTER VIII

LOCAL WORTHIES

IF ONE HAD TO NAME A DATE for the beginning of the mass popularity of the Lakes amongst tourists, one could not do better than take 1778, that of the first *Guide* to the district. One could make a long list of curious travellers before then, whilst even after that time they may for long have continued to be drawn from a rather restricted class. But hitherto, travellers have been individuals; henceforth, members of a crowd. A new movement begins to be 'in the air'.

The author was the learned and amiable Thomas West, who hides himself behind the description of 'Author of *The Antiquities of Furness*'. Born in Scotland in 1717 or 1720, in middle life he became a Jesuit, making the four vows in 1759. He was successively stationed at Holywell (Flintshire), at Ulverston, at Titup Hall near Dalton, and at Sizergh Hall, the seat of the Strickland family. One of the first principles of life in the country is that one does not wantonly give offence to one's neighbours, and even after his death a marked shade of discretion, natural enough at the time, will be noticed in the words of contemporaries, in avoiding mention of his priestly character. He died in 1779, the year following the publication of his *Guide*, and was buried at his own request in the family vault of the Stricklands in Kendal Parish Church.

This guide-book reveals the pastime of scenic tourism in the Lake District already settled into a cosy groove. The practice of conducting the reader to set 'stations' or viewpoints, and such a detail as that of the use of a plano-convex mirror (which antedated even Gray), and the style of illustration in the *Guide*, all show the picturesque routine as thoroughly well established. Gilpin, it is true, is never mentioned, but Gray's shadow has by now grown very long. The author follows humbly in his footsteps, offering pious commentary although frequently venturing to differ. But West is no doctrinaire. The personality which emerges from his book is that of a gentle-mannered classical scholar, not very enterprising in a physical sense, sedately pious, but affable, one who 'in the latter part of his life having much leisure time upon his hands, frequently accompanied genteel parties on the TOUR OF THE LAKES'.

For all that, he has the root of the matter in him. He unaffectedly loves natural scenery. Hear, then, the thoughts, staled by ten thousand repetitions since his day (if sincere expression can ever become stale) but with him at least fresh and simple:

Something new will open itself at the turn of every mountain, and a succession of ideas will be supported by a display of scenes behind scenes in endless perspective. The Contemplative traveller will be charmed by the sight of the sweet retreats that he will observe in these enchanting regions of calm repose; and the fanciful may figuratively review the hurry and bustle of busy life, in all its gradations, in the variety of unshaded rills that hang on the mountains' sides, the hasty brooks that warble through the dell, or the mighty torrents precipitating themselves at once with thundering noise from tremendous rocky heights; all pursuing one general end. . . .

Such as spend their lives in cities, and their time in crowds will here meet with objects that will enlarge the mind by contemplation, and raise it from nature to nature's first cause. Whoever takes a walk into these scenes, must return penetrated with a sense of the Creator's power, in heaping mountains upon mountains, and enthroning rocks upon rocks.

Unlike most of those who came after Gilpin, or those who needed to give their work some novelty by finding ways to differ from their predecessors, West's descriptions are not rendered monotonous by the doctrinaire spirit. The fact that a house was white did not prevent him enjoying its happy situation even though its conspicuousness might be open to criticism, under the stringent rules of the picturesque. He was the first to admire the typical Westmorland cottage with its slate roof and walls of undressed stone. Without romantic

prepossessions, he was willing to be pleased equally by cultivated or wild scenes, or by trees whether they were native
deciduous or the newly imported kinds of conifers. And
although for the assistance of his readers he recommended
set viewpoints, he was open-minded, and thus not a bore:
'To describe every picturesque view . . . would be an endless
labour. .. . . And, did language furnish expression, the
imagination would be fatigued with the detail. It is more
pleasing to speculative curiosity to discover of itself the
difference among such scenes . . . than to be informed of
them.' But what he and his genteel companions expected
to see was unquestionably the lakes and valleys, with the
woodland that garnished them and the rocks that diversified
them. The author did *not* like mountains, any more than
modern Friends of the Lake District like trees; and he made
no bones about it. The frequently-recurring words such as
'horrid' and 'hideous' might be thought merely a debt to
convention, or an attempt to wring out a pleasurable thrill;
but expressions like 'dreary' and 'dismal scene of barren-
ness' occur too often to leave us in any doubt. He *never* speaks
well of a mountain at close quarters, and urges no one to
climb them—not even Skiddaw. But, good man that he is,
he really prefers not to see them at all (unless as a distant
back-cloth) rather than be under the necessity of speaking
evil of them:

Ascend a steep hill surrounded with wood, and have a back view of
the lake. To the north is a most awful scene of mountains heaped upon
mountains, in every variety of horrid shape. Amongst them sweeps to
the north a deep winding chasm darkened by overhanging rocks, that
the eye cannot pierce, nor the imagination fathom; from which turn
your face to the east and have a view of Windermerewater.

Even Helvellyn, whose mild bulk for so many miles borders
the highroad from Grasmere to Keswick, is suspect: 'A
thousand huge rocks hang on Helvellyn's brow, which have
once been in motion, and are now seemingly prepared to
start anew.' But to be fair, West never indulges in sensationalism deliberately; at most he gives a little rein now and then

to his literary fancy, especially when warmed by recollections of classical imagery. When he is brought to close quarters with the more barren type of country, his tone is not unlike that of an experienced social worker constrained by his duty to mention the cruder facts of life. This is the way he introduces the simple and not very remarkable foot-track through the hills from Borrowdale to Langdale, by way of the Stake, which he calls 'an Alpine journey of a very extraordinary nature'. It is the only one of the kind that he gives his readers any encouragement to try:

Every part of nature has something to recommend it to the susceptible and ingenious. A walk or ride, on the summits of mountains, will afford a species of ideas, which, though often neither of the social nor luxuriant kind, will, nevertheless, greatly affect and entertain. . . . In a publication of this kind, a word or two respecting their nature and characteristic properties, seems as requisite as on several other subjects which are here discussed.*

But the necessity to refer to such matters should not be taken as condoning them:

Pike-a-Sticle is an inaccessible pyramidal rock, and commands the whole. Here Nature seems to have discharged all her useless load of matter and rock, when form was first impressed on chaos. . . . Beyond Langdale Chapel the vale becomes much more pleasing.

The question must naturally occur, just in what sense West and his clientele believed the Lakeland hills inaccessible. The Author would certainly not deceive us wantonly, from romantic or indeed from any other motives. But one ought not to expect too much from a rather sedentary scholar, no longer young. Just as we must unfeignedly value all humanity, despite useful and necessary differences of social degree, so the inanimate works of the Creator must no doubt be allowed to hold their ancient places, and be presumed to play their part in the great Scheme:

The middle regions are assumed by the flocks; and the upper regions (to man inaccessible) are abandoned to the birds of Jove. The shepherds

* West would have entirely agreed with the Scottish ghillie who, in the next century, described one of the finest corries of the Cuillin, in Skye, as 'a varra coorse rough place, with nae grazing in it. Nae fit place for a gentleman.'

only are conversant in the traditional annals of the mountains, and with all the secrets of the mysterious reign of chaos and old night; and they only can give proper information concerning their arcana; for others, who live within the shadows of these mountains, are often ignorant of their names.

From some humble friend, if not of his own discovery, West really knew the truth all the time, for on the fourth page of his book he says unequivocally: 'The mountains here are all accessible to the summit.'

There were few so poor-spirited as not to congratulate themselves on being superior to the notorious timidity of Gray, of whom no story could be too high-pitched. Even West says: 'Mr. Gray's account of Barrowside, and his relation of Borrowdale, are hyperboles, the sport of fancy he was pleased to indulge himselve in.' Gray had boggled even at the track in the valley of Borrowdale. West chides him for his timidity in not going all the way to Rosthwaite village (where as a matter of fact there was no road for wheeled vehicles at the date of Gray's visit).

James Clarke says Gray was so shocked at the awfulness of Skiddaw, as seen from Bassenthwaite, that he drew down the blinds of his carriage; also that after he had crossed Windermere ferry his courage was so far shaken on hearing that a disaster had once happened to the boat during the previous century, that he dared not return, except blindfold. Yet for all that, it is Gray who speaks like a prophet, and the others are merely guide-book hacks by comparison. Gilpin might coldly approve views, but Gray, however faltering his steps, unquestionably loved mountains.

For West it was perhaps natural to be a little lacking in human contacts. To him, a Scotsman, of Continental education, and ministering to the very few remaining Catholic families, the life of the shepherds was another world.

Provincial peculiarities and dialect were however just now attracting much attention, with genuine, because un-accustomed curiosity. The figure of the north-country native which emerges for us from the various 'specimens of the ancient dialect of the northern counties', and so on, which occur in this sort of book, strongly resembles what we know to-day, and seems generally much more real and credible than the countryman of Moreland or Wheatley's drawing. Not even the celebrated Mary of Buttermere acted up to the part assigned to her by the tourists; the northern character was proof, as a rule, against worse than this. To the next two writers we mention, Clarke and Budworth, the peasant appears neither arcadian nor an unfitting subject for polite notice, but very much as himself. Only a few more years were to go by, and the gush of warm human feeling which was one facet of the renewed romantic movement of the last years of the eighteenth century, changed all that, and moralising came in to falsify the picture.

The *Survey* produced in 1787 by James Clarke of Penrith was a very different book from the gentle West's. Clarke's was more or less a counterblast to the sentimental and picturesque writers, and perhaps most against West, whom he charged with magniloquence, and disregard of accuracy. 'This sublime way of writing,' he remarks surlily, 'is not in my province; a guide ought, in my opinion, to be merely narrative.' Thus speaks the Philistine. His own book is a rag-bag of anecdote, often scurrilous. His pose is that of the plain man, the knowledgeable Land Surveyor, the man with roots in practical experience and in local ancestry. Taking as his text the much vexed question of the house of Belle Isle he attacks the whole picturesque school.

The whole of this out-cry against regularity seems to me to have arisen from that cant style of painting which Gilpin and some others have introduced into writing. Not a tree, or shrub, or an old wall, but these gentlemen take measure of by the painter's scale; a poor harmless cow can hardly go to drink but they find fault with a want of grace in her attitude, or a horse drive away the flies with his tail . . . whoever examines these abortive nothings, which Mr. Gilpin calls landscapes, will hardly be able to trace one view, how well soever he may be acquainted with it: for my own part, they put me in mind of nothing so much as those landscapes and figures which boys fancy they see in the sky at sunset.

This criticism would not in the least have disturbed
Gilpin, who had made it fashionable to find for oneself in
nature exactly those effects which were already most admired
in painting, but possibly it militated against the fashionable
vogue of Clarke's own book.

Clarke himself had accompanied the artist Thomas Smith,
whose engravings could be obtained bound up with his own
Survey, but his appreciation of their purely artistic merits
was probably limited. He grudged the assumed knowledge
of his own district and the liberties taken with it, by its
newer admirers, however he might applaud their judgment
in coming to live and spend money in the country. Probably
he really despised much of the interest for which he set out
to cater: 'I have not attempted to please my readers by
laboured descriptions of beauties which do not exist.' By
comparison with the lore of the ways of foxes, eagles and deer,
and of fishing, the recent minor craze for scientific botany
struck such a man as a new-fangled and rather effeminate
subject: 'In that, I confess myself very ignorant, and can only
say that our plants are such as are common to other hilly
countries.'

He is proud of his own local ancestry and of the martial
spirit of the North, about which he has nearly as much to
say as about scenery:

In the Border Countries, every amusement, from the trifling plays of
children to the laborious sports of manhood, seems to have one uniform
tendency, I mean a tendency to train and inure the inhabitant to war
and danger.

The ruined tower, the subterraneous dungeon, the gloomy castle, are
so many monuments of the feudal system, and those days when no man
could sleep in any other security than what his valour and strength
procured him. . . . Every forest is the subject of tradition; the brave
actions of a few outlaws who lived upon the deer which then abounded,
are in every old woman's mouth, and these stories, as we have seen, are
often corroborated by undoubted facts.

But it seems the hardy moss-trooper of old brought nearly
as much gusto to legal wrangling about the disposal of booty,
under the Border Law, as to plundering itself.

He is not at all averse to stories about the oddities especially of the clergy, and dearly loves a history of a lawsuit or of a local grievance. Like a sagaman of old, he finds impartial satisfaction in exulting with the bold oppressive defendant and in resenting with the injured plaintiff. One gets a lifelike idea of his rather earthy and native personality, which was not without heartsome traits.

It is said that Clarke (perhaps to deceive his creditors) put about false rumours of his own death, just as afterwards did his distinguished fellow-Penrithian, the first Lord Brougham.

Clarke of course had his followers, even in his own day, and his rustic and philistine personality seems to accord with the rougher Corinthian tone which was ascendant in the war years and after. But the school of Gilpin was to have a long run yet.* The cult of the picturesque was never violently dethroned from popular approval, from that day to this, but has more or less just slowly faded away.

* As late as 1826 a pocket *précis* of Gilpin's dogmas was published under the title of *The Tourist's Grammar*.

CHAPTER IX

THE TOURISTS

THE FINEST WAY of entering the Lake District was perhaps that from Lancaster by the Sands. In saying this one does not forget the road from Tynedale, on which, at Hartside Cross, as one leaves behind the great sweeps of the Northumbrian moor, the whole western landscape bursts on the eye at once across the wide strath of the Eden far below. But none of the early travellers came this way, since in 1800 we are told that 'very seldom even a cart ventures to ascend the steeps of this Alpine pass' and it was only used by the farmers on horseback. A much more usual approach across the backbone of England, whether from the north-east or by the Great North Road, was by the majestic line of the Roman Road over Stainmore, with its descent through the foothills to sleepy dignified little Appleby. This was the historic route of the royal armies of the middle ages, to the Western Marches. As an alternative route from the south one could take the road from Leeds through Skipton, with its pleasant variety of park-land, river valleys, and distant hill views—just the thing for the eighteenth-century taste. The roads through Lancashire always had a bad reputation, being built of large cobblestones.

Before the railways, and before the growth of Lancashire, the more southerly routes had not the same relative importance as nowadays. Until Wordsworth had made Grasmere famous, and until the branch railway was constructed between Kendal and Windermere, it was Keswick, not the Rothay valley, which seemed to be the hub of the Lake District. Many tourists based themselves on the well-known inn at Ousebridge, at the northern outlet of Bassenthwaite, but this was closed early in the nineteenth century. In 1787 Ullswater had not yet a decent inn.

Buttermere, therefore, and even Ennerdale, were better known in the early days than Langdale, the head of which seemed, to de Quincey writing in the eighteen-thirties, an almost legendary region. Indeed it was a hundred years later before a road of smooth surface, above the level of the valley floor which was subject to floods, was built to its head. The western side of Cumberland was entirely undescribed by Thomas West; he says the roads were too bad to be recommended to tourists.

One way, it is good to know, the herd of motorists who take from others the enjoyment of that which they do not themselves appreciate, even yet cannot come. The discomforts and dangers of the passage of the Cartmel Sands may have left a gloomy recollection with some tourists, but, as one has so often felt, these very things must have made the objective of the journey seem better worth while.

On the vast levels of the Sands, the sense of isolation from the everyday world behind, and the spur to imagination furnished by the ring of blue hills in the distance, caused both West and Green to think this the best way of entering Lakeland for the first time. Perhaps these considerations are sentimental ones, and such an experienced traveller as Pennant (1772) was above them. 'A melancholy ride,' he says. 'The prospect on all sides quite savage, high barren hills indented by the sea, and dreary wet sands, rendered more horrible by the approach of night.' But though it is only manifest for a moment, beauty is often felt in similar cases, with a keenness which is not awake in comfortable surroundings. Gilpin would have gone that way, but for sheer lack of time. He had less than a week to see and judge the Lakes and to gather material for his book, so 'we were obliged to rest satisfied with forming imaginary pictures among the blue mists of the mountains'.

Three miles from Lancaster, the traveller embarked on the tidal sands at Hest Bank. He was guided over the fords by a salaried public officer who by long tradition, at least since the reign of Henry VIIIth, was known as the Carter, and was recognised by his being mounted on a white horse. Originally he had been a vassal of the great Abbey of Furness. His occupation is recollected by the names 'Carter Lane' and 'Carter House', which are still found, and this mediaeval officer himself crosses the sands at need to this day. By the time of Green's *Guide* a daily coach ran by the sands from Lancaster to Ulverston. None the less, the tides claimed the lives of one or two travellers upon the average, each year for centuries—frequently those who knew the fords well, and so took risks.*

And now for the activities of the tourist who has arrived. Thomas West himself was, more than any other known individual, the inventor of the recognised 'stations' or viewpoints, and perhaps of the word itself. At these stations, foreground and background were taken into account to present the most 'correct' combination. Their positions are most minutely described, for example, 'just to the left of the two ash trees and past the barn', and the tourist had only to follow these directions to see all that mattered. There was a right and a wrong direction in which to follow every recognised route, and even a pilot navigating an intricate passage at sea hardly needed to consider more carefully the position of the sun than the seeker after views. Apparently, to be led by the nose was exactly what the early tourist demanded. He was in a thoroughly serious frame of mind, as one not seeking any base sensual relaxation, but consciously a pilgrim of Taste—in plain words, an intellectual snob. The public was long since well broken in to these niceties of procedure,

* The passage across the combined estuaries of the little river Keer, and of the Kent, was of nine miles length. The channel of the former river, though smaller, was the most dangerous. Then, after crossing the Cartmel peninsula, across the estuaries of the Leven and Crake, issuing from Windermere and Coniston water respectively, the sands were again traversed for three miles to a point near the mouth of the present Ulverston Canal. The total distance from Lancaster to Ulverston was reckoned twenty miles. The present main road which goes by Levens Hall across the low-lying ground of Meathop to Newby Bridge was not built until much later, and the only alternative was therefore by way of Kendal, fully twice as far between Lancaster and Ulverston, besides being extremely hilly.

since scenery viewing was only landscape gardening on a larger scale, and it could be a social solecism of the first magnitude not to allow one's host to show one round his garden in the direction in which it was *designed* to be seen.

We must picture him armed with sketchbook, and with 'plano-convex mirror' as carried by Gray, and recommended by Gilpin. 'Where the objects are great and near it removes them to a due distance, and shows them in the soft colours of nature, and in the most regular perspective the eye can perceive or science demonstrate.' With the aid of this mirror and its appurtenances the tourist viewed scenery by turning his back on it, whilst vigorously exercising his intellectual faculties. A silver foil or a set of glasses of different colours was used, according to the light. Says a character in a contemporary comedy:

Speedwell, give me my glasses. Where's my Gray? By the bye, where's my Claude-Lorrain? I must throw a Gilpin tint over these magic scenes of beauty. (Looks through the glass.) How gorgeously glowing! Now for the darker. How gloomily glaring! Now the blue. (Pretends to shiver with cold.) How frigidly frozen! The effect is inexpressibly interesting. The amphitheatrical perspective of the long landscape; the peeping points of the many coloured crags of the headlong mountains, looking out most interestingly from the picturesque luxuriance of the bowery foliages margining their ruggedness, and feathering the fells; the delightful differences of the heterogeneous masses; the horrific mountains, such scenes of ruin and privation; the outrageous and reposing hue of the copsey lawns, so touchingly beautiful; the limpid lapse of Lowdore, are so many circumstances of imagery, which altogether combine a picture which for its sentimental beauty and assemblages of sublimity I never exceeded in the warmest glow of my fancied descriptions.

There is really something to be said for such painstaking methods. The music-lover at least will appreciate the argument that one might as well expect to extract the full benefit from music whilst somnolently munching sandwiches in the back seat of a moving saloon car with the radio turned on, as expect to enjoy visual beauties from the same point of vantage.

Apropos of plano-convex mirrors, it is encouraging to be

reminded of the multitude of the forgotten minor pleasures of life awaiting rediscovery at need. When there was no question of the option of another visit next week-end, people were keen to exploit to the full all that was offered, and so perhaps got as much benefit out of a very limited visit as the regular week-ender does in years. In the list of well-recognised pleasures was also included: being melancholy among ruins. These were the sort of things done by smart people anxious to be up-to-date, or rather, by highbrow persons trying out the diversions which smart people would in due course wish to imitate.

Miss Beccabunga Veronica (the comedy character already quoted) was, as her name implies, a botanist. This pursuit seems to have become fashionable in its new, Linnaean form, at least a couple of decades before scientific classification of rocks became to a similar degree familiar to the ordinary educated man. For the latter development, 1820 may be taken as an approximate commencing-date. The sacrifice of the old conceptions of geology involved the loss of the cataclysmic or 'sublime' fables which had contributed so much to the enjoyment of earlier travellers.* Jonathan Otley of Keswick did much, about 1820, towards the debunking of the local bogeys. He gave the coup de grâce to the legend of the 'Bottom Wind' of Derwentwater, which had been thought to be due to some volcanic agency, and also to the belief that Blencathra mountain was an ancient volcano, of which the shape of the crater was represented by the coombe of Purple Tarn. (The author of the descriptions prefixed to Fielding and Walton's elegant series of aquatints, published in 1820, still subscribed to the old theory about Purple Tarn.) From these scientific advances it followed that from this time onward there must be a divorce between the school which wanted romantic thrills, and those who preferred to keep up the appearance of being scientific students. And in the days

* The issue of the painful collision with the Book of Genesis which thus became inevitable, was not finally decided for the general public until the eighteen-sixties.

WASTWATER   by T. H. A. Fielding, 1821

DUNMAIL RAISE

Etching by W. F. Wells, 1810, after the drawing by the Rev. Joseph Wilkinson. This
series of drawings by Wilkinson was published to the accompaniment
of text by Wordsworth forming the early editions of the *Description*.

AMBLESIDE, LOOKING NORTH TO THE SALUTATION INN   by William Green, 1822

The gates of the artist's house (which still stands) are at left foreground

of their novelty, scientific pursuits were just as fashionable as had been the tastes which they succeeded. We should also mention the agricultural improvers, of whom Arthur Young was the chief. He visited the Lakes in the last decade of the eighteenth century. A map showing the surface geology or soils was a feature of Housman's *Guide* of 1800.

Not everyone of course was a naturalist. For the social-minded and the hearty, this was the age of picnics and puns; of music-parties by the water, and of abusing the revolutionary French. And how they picnicked! The universal practice of taking guides, besides being perhaps a tribute to the social position of the travellers, may be explained in part by the problem of transporting to the scene of action the indispensable provisions: the huge meat and fruit pasties, the roast fowls with their garnishings, and the bottles of wine. Holding this sort of feast among lovely scenery no doubt appealed to the dramatic instinct of those who had wearied of the banditti-cum-ruin theme. In the Age of Sentiment, the gentle West had ventured to suggest only July and August as suitable months for a tour. For the mentally and physically aggressive nineteenth-century tourist, Green recommended May, June and September in addition. As early as 1787, it was apparently not unusual for visitors to live the summer through in marquees, which were no doubt, since Clarke mentions them with approval, of a sort to be a credit and a profit to the local tradespeople. Pyne's engravings show them still in vogue in the eighteen-fifties.

From 1780 onwards there were the regattas on Bassenthwaite, and also on Derwentwater, culminating in the sham naval attack on Pocklington's island. They were followed by sports, including wrestling (which took place 'after the ladies retired'). As the extreme naturalistic movement represented by Payne Knight's followers reached a momentary dominance at the very end of the century, this jollification was rather frowned upon as disrespectful to the majesty of nature, and, by the romantic, as probably uncongenial to the shade of the hermit, St. Herbert. After being held

F

regularly until 1791, the regattas were discontinued, and only revived in 1825, as a show for Sir Walter Scott and George Canning, on the occasion of their almost-royal visit. By this time the missionary zeal of the Lakers had lost its first keen austerity, whilst the sense of public pageantry, in harmony with national self-congratulation upon victory, and with the classical revival in art, was strong.

CHAPTER X

REFLECTIONS SUGGESTED BY THE CONTEMPLATION OF THE SUBLIME

MOUNTAINS had, by the end of the eighteenth century, managed to attract some extraneous senti- ment to themselves, since, as Leslie Stephen pointed out, they had become to some extent a favourite symbol of the left wing in politics, and so continued at least down to the time of Shelley. Thus, Payne Knight winds up his poem *The Landscape* with a survey of the French Revolution, which otherwise would seem rather uncalled for. This association of ideas is hard to explain, except by recalling that the idea of human nature being superior to then-existing political institutions, and the idea of the intuitive effect of natural scenery, were, historically, born about the same period. No doubt the struggles of Paoli and the Corsicans, or later, of Hofer and the Tyrolese against Napoleon, or even traditions of the earlier Vaudois and the Camisards, as well as the Vicaire Savoyard, had much to do with it. After the nine- teenth-century reforms had reduced liberty from an aspira- tion to a matter of familiar and tedious political machinery, or of rioting in cities, this train of thought died a natural death.

Far-fetched as they may seem at the first impression, still other sentiments crowd themselves into notice alongside those we have mentioned. If the awfulness of waterfalls, the peacefulness of lakes, the rumbling of winds could regularly and naturally suggest thoughts about political liberty, they also, as often as not, could set going trains of reflection which ended with such subjects as family affection, being grateful for one's daily food, and charity to the poor.

At any rate all these things were fashionable topics about the same time. Miss Veronica, in the comedy, is made to give money to the blind beggar in Keswick market-place, and to enter the fact, with full stylistic honours, in her journal. At any time after about 1800, our tourist might lend interest to his drive over Honister Pass by going to stare at a young woman at Buttermere who had been the victim of a rather commonplace story of seduction and desertion. (After a time, there was the risk of a certain anticlimax here, since many tourists failed at first to recognise their fanciful mental picture in the stout, prosaic countrywoman who had waited on them at the village alehouse.)

The delighted self-consciousness, the total lack of embarrassment, is what strikes us most. One can only try to conjure up for oneself the contemporary conditions which made such a mental attitude possible. Just as in the case of the political radicalism above mentioned, we must imagine all these feelings so new as to be not yet 'sicklied o'er with the pale cast of thought', not yet contaminated by dismal reflection about the pedantries of economics, by sectarian bickering, or the blundering machinery of social legislation which necessarily attended the practical working out of these motives—a moment, one may add, when there was a pleasurable thrill, and one worth entering in a diary, even in the act of throwing litter about the countryside, as one fears Wordsworth implies that he did in his *Excursion to Scafell Pike*.

A trait, however, which one cannot miss in the early tourists, before as well as after Wordsworth, is the way in which they one and all associate natural scenery intimately with religion. To do so was, for many of them, far from being merely a due paid to convention, whatever it may have become later, by force of repetition.

To Gray, every torrent, every precipice, had seemed pregnant with religion and poetry. The waterfalls, said Hutchinson, excited the most solemn strains of meditation. To Green it seemed 'mountains of such varied forms and hues fill the mind with the most pleasingly solemn sensations, and in a survey of the scenes surrounding him the spectator cannot but contemplate with religious awe, the wonders of his beneficent Creator'. But it is needless to quote more; one could find examples of the same kind from almost any of the amateurs of scenery; in the scope of this book it was usually the awe-inspiring, rather than the merely agreeable, in nature which suggested such thoughts. If we nowadays fail to associate natural beauty instinctively with religious feeling it is ourselves who are exceptional—probably such thoughts would occur spontaneously to the youths who attend the fortnightly courses of training at the Mountain Training Schools if their paramilitary syllabus does not keep them too busy. Perhaps such notions occur to them when they get home, at the tranquillity of their workbench. But most of all is treasured in memory the moment snatched from hard exertion or anxiety.

One may, however, find it hard to see why, in principle, so much inert stone and water, no matter on what scale of size, should suggest religious ideas more inherently belonging to the spiritual or personal plane, and particularly since the aspect of mountains which most forcibly struck our great-grandfathers was that of ruin and chaos, not of design. 'The ruins of an earlier world' was how Coruisk struck Scott, whilst the Borrowdale fells reminded Gray of the poet's phrase 'Chaos and old Night'. Few, in the Romantick Age, comment on the appearances of order in nature such as the delicate patterning of crystals; whilst the vast conceptions of geological change, which were to come into conflict with the chronology of the Book of Genesis, were not yet formed.

On the other hand, a modern author has questioned whether the feeling for the beauty of scenery is capable of a material explanation. How, he asks, can the capacity for such a feeling have been produced, on a merely mechanistic view of evolution—and if not, must it not point to some transcendental truth? But surely in explaining evolutionary phenomena, greater difficulties than this are met with?

To explain the connection, one must revert to the distinction between the qualities which used respectively to be

known as The Beautiful and The Sublime. For us to-day
'beauty' has a much more comprehensive and vague meaning than it had for the men of the early romantick period.
In their sense of the words, it was not Beauty, but Sublimity,
which they came to the Lake District to see. Both of these
are included in the word beauty as we use it now, as well as
a third element, the picturesque; this last simply a quality
of craftsmanlike taste such as a painter would make use of
in measuring the proportions of the ingredients of beauty
and of sublimity to be included in a painting, much as a
cook might measure the proportions of sugar and spice in a
sauce. For us too, 'beauty' carries the burden of a hundred
and fifty additional years of theory and of propaganda, of
épatisme and of aestheticism.

Under the heading of The Beautiful, there were normally
included only those things which had a tendency to nourish,
to comfort, and the like, rather than to excite or shock. Here
is Uvedale Price's illustration of a beautiful landscape, un-
mixed with anything picturesque:

> But suppose . . . he was to enter a glade, or small valley of the softest
> turf and finest verdure, the ground on each side swelling gently into
> knolls, the whole adorned with trees of the smoothest and tenderest bark,
> and most elegant forms, mixed with tufts of evergreens and flowering
> shrubs; All these growing as luxuriantly as in garden mould . . . whilst a
> natural path way led the eye amidst all these intricacies. Suppose a clear
> and gentle stream to flow through this retirement on a bed of the purest
> gravel pebbles. . . .

and so on.

It does not on these lines seem difficult to account on a
mechanistic basis for the evolution of the sense of The
Beautiful, since ultimately it amounted precisely to what had
survival value or tended to the propagation of the species.
The Sublime, on the other hand, answers to the equally
familiar need of the living organism, whether less or more
highly developed, for stimulus and exertion, no matter
whether on its physical, mental or spiritual plane. By
definition, The Sublime is anything the vision of which awes

one; awes one by its evident power to destroy if one should venture upon too close contact. Such a feeling of awe is appropriate alike to impending crags ready to topple on one's head, or to the sensations of a prophet on Mount Sinai, confronting the God of the Old Testament. What one has to consider, perhaps, is just which psychological need it was, for which eighteenth-century enlightenment, or eighteenth-century protestantism, failed to provide adequately. For if any less bold hypothesis offers itself, one hardly dare suggest that it is human nature which alters much. What does alter is the jumbled heritage of prejudices having their origin in circumstances, and constituting the 'outlook' of a period. The obvious difference between the Tourists and ourselves is, that mountain scenery would strike them with a more forcible sense of awe by reason of their being less accustomed to it. We have to consider, too, not only what our ancestors may actually have felt on viewing grand scenery but how far their education had prepared them to acknowledge and express such feelings. For all that, many of us, by casting our minds back to childhood, can remember experiencing impressions as powerful as those of the Tourists.

CHAPTER XI

HOBNAILS AND HUMANITY

A NEW TYPE, numerous enough to be noticeable half a decade or so before the beginning of the nineteenth century, was the pedestrian tourist, who was 'discovered' for the benefit of a London audience in *The Lakers, a Comic Opera*. Not indeed that people did not believe in the possibility of accomplishing a tour afoot, but it was left to those of a certain rather humble status. The pedestrian is described as dressed in sailor's short jacket and long trousers. 'The dress is light, and well adapted for travelling.' He had a certain amount of prejudice to overcome at first, and his motives for travelling were liable to be miscontrued, at a time when the thousands of discharged sailors and soldiers who had small provision made for them must often have had little resource but vagrancy and crime. A certain slightly defiant aloofness might be needed in an age when people were for various reasons even more afraid of not appearing to do the right thing in the eyes of innkeepers, waiters, and so on, than they are nowadays—the same sort of courage Mrs. Bloomer later needed when introducing her rational costume for female cyclists.

As befits pioneers who consciously challenged social usage, the pedestrians are made for dramatic purposes to speak with a distinctly priggish tone:

We trust, sir, that we are gentlemen, though thus habited, and taking our tour on foot to gain knowledge of our country and of mankind.

Pedestrian! How picturesque too their appearance! I have often heard of many who travel in this *rational* way, but was never so fortunate as to be acquainted with any. . . . But a'nt you afraid of being taken up?

'No, we injure no one, why should anyone injure us?' they reply, an echo of Rousseau in their tones. The pedestrian

slightly disapproves of most of the ordinary manners and
customs he sees around him;

> We will still, our aim pursuing,
> for improvement travel on.
> Men and manners still be viewing
> making all we see our own.
> We not envy power or riches,
> We have pleasures, we have health
> and experience fully teaches
> these alone are solid wealth.

One of the first to describe a really pedestrian holiday was
Joseph Budworth, who wrote as 'The Rambler'. He visited
the Lakes in 1792, and again in 1799. He had spent most of
his life up till then (he was 39) in soldiering abroad. The
long voyage to the East cut a man off from his family for
half a lifetime, and a soldier's bonds with his messmates
became the strongest of all. The Rambler is continually
breaking off to reminisce about his army days and dear lost
comrades. But, unlike the Lakers, he was not a sententious
prig, come to demonstrate his theories. The conditions of
Service life seem to have produced a type of man not unlike
the Jolly Jack Tar of tradition: open, artless, generous, with
a fine unembarrassed way with the girls, fond of humour and
homely rhetoric, whilst disclaiming subtlety of all kinds.
'Whatever I have written comes warm from the imagination, with the views full before it. . . . I have no fine houses,
no fine paintings, no compliments to great people to swell
out my book with.' Though he loves the 'beautifully misshapen' mountain country, he is not the least bit 'picturesque'
—he would probably have got on well enough with Clarke,
once the latter had thawed off his initial suspicion of him as
a foreigner. Budworth enjoys the Fifth Freedom, the Freedom
from Cant, and there is an immediacy about his babblings
which is very captivating: 'Just under' (the top of Helvellyn)
'is Red Tarn, shaped like a Bury Pear—if I had a draught of
it, it would be worth all the fruit in the world, for my tongue
cleaves to the roof of my mouth.'

On one visit, he walked 240 miles in the fortnight, and he
was a pretty stout hill-climber too. Skiddaw, of course, had
for many years past been considered an ordinary enough
excursion. Clarke gives directions for finding the approach:
'. . . the rivulet which falls down at Armathwaite near Dr.
Brownrigg's house, and then a green path conveys us almost
to the top of Skiddaw . . . this way a horse can travel.' The
romantic novelist Mrs. Radcliffe described her ascent in the
same year as Budworth, with every intention, obviously, of
extracting a thrill from it, but all she can seriously complain
of is the thin-ness of the air. Her narrative cannot be taken
as any true reflection of the common attitude. One of the
last to affect an exaggerated physical susceptibility to the
effects of mountain-walking was de Quincey.

Budworth did a good deal more than Skiddaw; his bag
included Helvellyn, Coniston Old Man, Helm Crag and the
Langdale Pikes. The last two named, he was (so far as the
record goes, and quite probably in fact) the first tourist to
climb. Everyone took guides in those days—even 30 years
after, so wild a spirit as Christopher North, who was
accustomed to bivouacking in the Scottish Highlands. Of
course there were no maps of any use for the purpose, but
before the taste for mountain walking was widely shared,
and comrades easily got, there was a lot to be said for taking
a guide merely as a companion, or for his local anecdotes.
Or can it be a matter of the ancient popular tradition of the
foot hunt, or of the stranger's business being everybody's
business, just as it still is in Ireland, as against the Late
Victorian donnish habit of wandering lonely as a cloud (or
just with one's own coterie) whilst thinking high thoughts
that would not interest the Great Unwashed? But William
Wordsworth, so far as he is recorded as making ascents of
the higher hills, which was not very often, took guides too.

The Rambler, energetic as he was, was not at all happy
on steep ground. This is odd, in a man who had been
stationed on the Rock of Gibraltar. But he did not have the
specially nailed boots we now have, and consequently had

to rely a good deal on his spiked stick, similar to those the
shepherds carried. The loss of his arm, in warfare, would not
help him. His guide led him straight down from the top of
Helvellyn to the road, a mile beyond the old Cherry Tree
Inn (itself not far north of Wythburn Chapel). 'I would not,
whilst descending, have looked at anything but my feet for
all the prospect in the universe.' And descending the Langdale Pikes, 'when we had got a good way down, we had to
pass over a large bulging part of the mountain, across a
sward nearly perpendicular, and of an immoderate height . . .
by a sheep track. . . .' Here Budworth simply could not bear
the airy outlook, and bandaged his right eye. It has been
suggested that this was actually on Jack's Rake, which is
nowadays regarded as a scramble or climb, although a very
easy one, a narrow ledge slanting across the face of a cliff,
but the specific description seems to me absolutely to
preclude this, and it was probably merely on steep grass.
Moreover, if Budworth had really been on Jack's Rake, this
is not at all the style in which he would have described it.

There is another curious story in Clarke, of a Mr. Hasell,
the squire of Dalemain, near Ullswater. Whilst foxhunting
on the top of Swarth Fell

his eagerness threw him into a situation that rendered it impossible to
return. He therefore dismounted, and pressed as close as possible to his
horse; thus supporting each other through this perilous stage, they
arrived safe at the bottom in the presence of many spectators, and where
no person was ever known before or since to have descended.

The suggestion that he was indebted to his horse for
extricating him from precipitous ground is one of those odd
bits of evidence which make one almost doubt whether
people's bodily and mental powers were of the same kind
as to-day. But of course he had to save his horse, and it is
merely the teller of the story who has got it a little muddled,
as to the respective shares of credit.

This Rambler of ours (at the time at least of his Lake
District book) made no pretensions to be, nor was he, a
literary artist. He has no idea at all of building up his effects;

he does not even develop his thumb-nail sketches properly. He is continually breaking off to mention acquaintances in Gibraltar, or the robin that used to perch on his fishing-rod at home in Surrey, or just to remark that the wind was as rough as 'on a certain day fifteen years ago which I well remember', but he never thinks of putting us in the picture. Most bad writers are bad, however, not because they are without art, but because being in varying degrees subconsciously aware of their own deficiency, they strive to compensate it by dogmatism, floridity, repetitiveness, stylisation, or what-all. It is just this complexity which makes them so fascinating to the connoisseur. So, when Budworth says, 'Whatever I have written comes warm from the imagination, with the views full before it' we sigh gently, recognising, as we think, the familiar battle-cry of the perfectionist 1780s, the horns of Utopia faintly blowing, and prepare for a page or two of gush. But we are wrong in our expectation. Budworth would not know how even if he wanted. But if he is not remarkable as a writer, he is quite uncommonly human as a man. Without the slightest affectation, he likes his fellow men, and is interested in them, and can talk to them on level terms—not like the Friend of Humanity talking to the Needy Knife Grinder. He looks at the complexions of the children in the slums of Kendal, and wonders sympathetically about their health, without the least implied self-congratulation for his kindness of heart or observation. He will forget the whole Lake District for two pages if he meets an old comrade in poor circumstances. He talks like a nice uncle to the girl at Buttermere. He estimates that the strolling players at Keswick only took thirty-six shillings, and is sorry. 'I was awoke by the sound of a fiddle from the next alehouse. I threw up my window with a determination to be pleased at what kept me awake.' He stumbles into a quarry at night because he has had 'one over the eight' and is quite honest about it; equally without any bravado. His friendly interest extends even to sheep: '. . . descending about two hundred yards, came to a charming spring, with many sheep about it, surrounded by a small plot of the liveliest verdure, which must be a nibbling treasure to them; we will suppose they hold their *conversaziones* here.'

This readiness to be pleased, to meet people or sheep on perfectly level terms, without any *arrière-pensée*, makes some of his dialogue passages astonishingly authentic. Ours is a book about the development of ideas, not about people any more than it is about the Lake District scenery as such. The value to us of this genial, canny Midlander is his positive evidence that good nature and good sense were exactly the same commodities, irrespective of social class or locality, in the eighteenth century as at any other time. It is as though there was suddenly a gap in the curtains of the dim and stuffy room of literature, and the outside daylight showed us a few of Thomas Gray's simple children of nature as live people.

One of the earliest science-fiction stories, Jules Verne's perhaps, or Conan Doyle's, tells us of a ray which could pierce not only through space but through time. Budworth's ray, by amazing luck, not only lights up for us the first tourist in the act of setting foot on the now so much frequented Langdale Pikes, but, simultaneously, the first authentic utterance of the simple native: 'I'th neome oh fackins, wot a broughtin you here?' 'Curiosity,' replied the Rambler. 'I think you mun be curious enough. I neor cum here but efter runaway sheop, an' I'm then so vext at um, I cud throa um deawn th'Poike.'

But there are other ghosts we have to interview, who do not enjoy the same luck, and we cannot allow them to be frightened away. Ideas have to be looked for in books, and libraries are places for work. So draw the curtains again, trim the candles—not that we would use them if we had more efficient lighting for the purpose—and reach for the next book on the dusty top shelf.

CHAPTER XII

NATURE RE-BORN:
THE NINETEENTH CENTURY

AT THE BEGINNING OF THE CHAPTER in which Gilpin was mentioned, allusion was made to the gradual disposition to turn towards country pursuits, and to simpler, freer, more candid manners.

During all the eighteenth century 'nature' had been one of the hardest worked of words. To Pope she was a rhetorical invocation, which might conveniently bear any meaning or none; to Johnson a provincial hoyden, of more than doubtful orthodoxy; to Gray a sophisticated nymph, who was not to be cross-examined too strictly about her sentiments.

Gilpin had felt for her the romantic passion of ignorance, and had asked of her the mysterious and sensational. Now, though still a goddess, she was found to be as familiar and simple in her tastes as the Monarch, George III, himself. Her inspired priests were the poor—industrious or otherwise —the Leech Gatherer, and the Idiot Boy, and through the mouth of Wordsworth they were now to speak in their own persons. Gray professed no illusions about the natives who lived most closely in contact with the scenes he ardently admired: with his callow undergraduate insolence, he could say of the natives of the Savoy Alps: 'The creatures that inhabit them are, in all respects, below humanity.' (He was, for politeness' sake, more disposed to subscribe to the Arcadian myth where his own countrymen were concerned.)

But to Wordsworth, it appeared that 'in the condition of life our elementary feelings co-exist in a state of greater simplicity . . . the manners of rural life germinate from those elementary feelings, and . . . in that condition the passions of men are incorporated with the beautiful and permanent forms of nature. . . .' It is because of this, he says, that the language of the poor and rustic is the best suited for poetry, and it is on the model of their lives, it seems, that the poet should approach nature. The poet 'considers man and nature as essentially adapted to each other, and the mind of man as naturally the mirror of the fairest and most interesting qualities of nature'.

He did not hold that nature only spoke by her sublime and terrible aspects. In this he differed from the romanticks who preceded him, and whose taste was for stronger drugs. 'A stranger to mountain scenery naturally on his first arrival looks out for sublimity in every object that admits of it, and is almost always disappointed.' 'The craving for prospect, immoderate particularly in new settlers', was one of the chief reasons why they so often disfigured the landscape by their building. In any case, the appreciation of picturesque scenery was an art, and 'an accurate taste in it, as in poetry, and all the other arts, as Sir Joshua Reynolds has observed, is an acquired talent, which can only be produced by thought and a long-continued intercourse with the best models'. In holding this last view (which he twice repeats) Wordsworth does no more than follow Gilpin. But the acquirement of this new-fangled and rather self-conscious art was not essential, since the power according to one's opportunities to absorb moral lessons direct from nature was inborn, and within the reach of the humblest. Gilpin had written for the upper middle class, for those who, whilst unable to practice large-scale landscape gardening on their own account, could yet bear the very considerable expense of a post-chaise in quest of the picturesque. It needed whole decades after the establishment of railways for the appreciation of scenery to become a commonplace, among the public generally. Wordsworth regarded the votaries of the art with suspicion for their dilettantism. Nothing could be further from his desire than to play the ecstatic, drugging himself with romantic sensation. If Gilpin is taken as a typical romantic then we can scarcely use the same word of Wordsworth.

But the latter's mind, as we frequently find, operated with an almost Gladstonian subtlety especially as regards the practical consequences of his views: he could concede nature's influence on mankind without wishing for contact with those influenced; he could declare the need for seeking her guidance without feeling obliged to welcome the acceptance of his ideas by the multitude or by any particular class. One is well advised to remember that he (as has also been said of the Laws of England), generally holds in reserve a qualification to every principle he enunciates, and generally one that is entirely reasonable and difficult to refute.

The curious tone, precise and flat, in the prose style of the beginning of the nineteenth century is characteristic: so cold to us, so fresh in its not-unselfconscious simplicity when first it took its vogue. It is this which expresses and calls attention to the almost abrupt change of spiritual climate which seems to occur co-incidently with the turn-over from the eighteenth to the nineteenth century. Likewise is the artistic taste of the period: classical, massive, and cold.

The new tone, to our ears so prim and prosaic, is evident on a humble level in William Green, the artist, who worked at Ambleside from 1800 to 1823. One recognises it clearly in the preface to his early book of *Studies*. Even his diction and prose cadences bespeak it:

The artist . . . feels he has a right to lay claim to characteristic accuracy. He has always considered that fidelity of imitation is the first step to improvement in the fine arts, and that those who have not originally attended with painful correctness, to the minutiae of nature, must be very ill qualified to form those grand ideal compositions, which, unless they are founded upon, and connected by an intimate knowledge of truth, are indeed but as:

> a tale
> told by an idiot, full of sound and fury
> signifying nothing.

ENNERDALE LAKE

by William Westall, 1822

LEATHES WATER (LOOKING NORTH)   by William Green, 1820

—a severe but hardly unfair description of the earlier romantic movement, of which it might serve as the epitaph.

Green, who was born in 1760 in Manchester, first visited the Lakes as assistant to Yates in his cartographical survey of Lancashire. Here he met West, already author of the *Antiquities of Furness* and now just publishing his *Guide*, who encouraged him to begin painting as an amateur. Some years afterwards Green undertook a very careful survey of Manchester, the first ever to be made, but its publication was forestalled in 1793 by an inferior production. Partly in disappointment, partly in accordance with his developing tastes, he gave up surveying and turned to painting and etching.

Green was not a great artist, and his writings, as for example his *Guide*, except for set passages like that quoted, have the inconsecutive style of an unpractised writer. But if not merely as an outstandingly sincere and lovable man, yet because he is the pioneer of a new spirit so far as the Lake District delineation is concerned, he is worthy to mark a stage in our story. His output of etchings and aquatints was enormous, running into four figures.

No one before him is near his like for detailed and wide-ranging knowledge of the country. The reason for his very limitations lay in his conscientiousness, his modesty, his pleasure in recording what he saw. He insists that it was not his aim to concoct a picture in imitation of abstract or current academic models, but to divest himself as far as possible of all style whatever. That of course was scarcely within his power. This is a movement away from the factitious elements in the picturesque, although he never quite escapes some of the commonplace artifices of his predecessors, for example, the three sheep or cows to help out the composition, and the familiar division of foreground, middle and background. His drawings would be much more interesting to us if they did not exclude the human element so completely. He has little variety of treatment. Too often he repeated the rather heavy foreground of trees, the

G

deliberately tame hill-profiles beyond. He is at his best in his *Studies,* of single objects: boulders, trees, and cottages, where fresh interest in structure enabled him to improve on current methods.

Unlike Gilpin, he does not feel the need of constantly asking himself what the country would look like seen through the eyes of Salvator Rosa or even the benign Claude —though he may sometimes be weak enough to allow his reader to understand he has heard their names—or through a selection of tinted viewing glasses. He has too much integrity to pretend he imagines catastrophes of nature awaiting the traveller at every turn. He at least knew that it was only shepherds, and not brigands, who were to be met with in the lonely dales or among the crags.

Though he does not mention the name of Humphrey Repton, Green's favourite landscapes are obviously Reptonian. Their traits are indefiniteness and gradation, avoidance of appearance of formal design, abundance of trees, especially native ones, which displayed the softer shapes. A division of land-ownership, he thought, conduced to the most pleasing kind of landscape, as there was less uniformity and at the same time there was less interference with nature. Ambleside was for this reason more beautiful than the neighbourhood of Rydal Hall. Above all (following Gilpin and Repton), trees with pointed tops or unusual colourings, as well as peaked mountains, must be regarded with jealous suspicion. He is especially Reptonian in his manner of employing woodland. It should not be uniform or thick, as a thick wood seen from a distance merely repeated the contours of the ground. Nor should it altogether impede the outlook, though as far as possible it should hide completely every man-made object which did not imitate nature. A wood might still serve its purpose if it were thinned to the extent of nine out of ten, or even nineteen out of twenty. The transition from the more solid masses to the more open treatment should always be gradual. By the judicious use of wood either the offensive features in the landscape (and

to the person of 'correct taste' these could be many) might
be masked, or even the disagreeable shape of a mountain
apparently modified. It followed that the particular feature
or local ornament such as the 'Arno's Vale' (at Shenstone's
Leasowes) or any special effect which, by offering itself as
an object of sentiment or of artistic admiration demanded
definite treatment, was seldom now attempted.

Green's opinions and his countless and very tedious verbal
descriptions of particular places may be best understood if
considered as practical applications of Repton's ideas, like
Repton's own 'riders' or sketches of layouts. The impression
of monotony in the wider landscapes Green drew is thus not
quite unintended, and the trees in the foregrounds (which
are often so uninterestingly drawn by comparison with his
proved power of draughtsmanship) are perhaps intentionally
merely symbols of Reptonian Foreground Tree.

The opinion of the educated classes about landscape
picturesqueness was every bit as strong, and also, though
faced with less potent enemies, fully as effective as to-day's.
It will be guessed that it was not every Lakeland scene which
would earn the applause of the landscape critic. Derwentwater, as a whole, Green considered 'at the present time
more captivating to the untutored than to the tutored eye'.
This censure was principally earned by the methods of
afforestation, and the recent felling which had taken place.
Green actually adopts Payne Knight's depreciatory remarks
about the lake, already quoted.

The planners of this period certainly did not usually
shrink from large conceptions or large undertakings. 'To
render to Derwentwater beauties it may formerly have
possessed, would demand an extraordinary degree of attention to the land on its borders.' It would indeed!—'all its
picturesque localities . . . and all the avenues to them, and
to the rocks seen beyond them, by a well-considered and
tasteful reduction of the trees' were to be 'brought into a
composition grand, solemn, and particularly interesting'. He
writes for those who had before them a lifetime of wealth

and peace, to spend in planning the growth of new planta-
tions which should produce the precise effect required; and
more indeed, for there is always an implied rebuke to those
who expect to see the results of their labour in their own
lifetime.

Amid all this, one cannot miss recognising Green's deep
love for every stone of the fells and dales, based on full
acquaintance of them in all conditions. 'For his own part,
indeed, were the writer asked whether he should prefer a
month of fair or rainy weather he would not hesitate to
declare for the rainy month.' He was the first to draw
Duddondale; except for a crude engraving in Housman's
Guide, the first to draw Wasdale. He it was who first urged
people to visit Western Cumberland, and Langdale, too,
which for a long while was one of the least accessible and
least visited of the dales. His many years of mountain
excursions on foot, in all weathers, put to shame the week
or fortnight which a Gilpin, or a Hutchinson, had thought
enough for a book.

In 1817, in failing health, he writes: 'The author would sell
the accumulated and progressive study of seventeen past
summers, to be enabled to draw and paint out of doors in
all seasonable weather for three years from the present time.'
If not to those who rushed through the land in post-chaises,
expecting to have all the choicest secrets of nature revealed
to them in a week by arrangement with innkeepers, at least
to Green was granted that which Wordsworth promised to
the pensive spirits who should live humbly with nature. In
the words of his friend Christopher North: 'Green—kind,
courteous, ingenious, and enthusiastic spirit—farewell.'

In the technicalities of landscape theory, Wordsworth also
belonged to the school of Repton; or at least he started from
Repton, however he may have transcended him. Wordsworth's own intense and cultivated personal sensibility, by
means of what he called Imagination, is something very
different from Repton's trade of landscape-upholstery. He is
therefore at all times liable to burst the bounds of merely

'correct' picturesque taste. Thus, having declared (with orthodoxy) that conspicuous white houses disfigure a landscape, he proceeds to hedge:

> I do not, however, mean to deny that a small white building . . . may, in some situations, be a delightful and animating object. . . . On the sides of bleak and desolate moors, we are indeed thankful for the sight of white cottages and white houses plentifully scattered . . . this is said, however, with hesitation, and with a wilful sacrifice of some higher enjoyments.

And indeed, he nearly always lived in a white, or at best roughcast, house himself.

Unlike Gilpin, and even Green, Wordsworth generally knows too well how complex natural beauty is, to attempt to lay down simple recipes for its attainment, or lightly to attempt a complete description of it. Thus, in giving a warning against the excessive appetite for 'sublimity', he says, 'The principal charm of the smaller waterfalls consists in certain proportions of form and affinities of colour, among the component parts of the scene', and, speaking of the defacement of scenery, he says:

> All gross transgressions of this kind originate, doubtless, in a feeling natural and honourable to the human mind, viz. the pleasure which it desires from distinct ideas, and from the perception of order, regularity, and contrivance. . . . But I would beg of those who are eager to create the means of such gratification, first carefully to study what already exists, and they will find . . . an abundant variety of forms marked out with a precision that will satisfy their desires. Moreover, a new habit of pleasure will be formed opposite to this, arising out of the perception of the fine gradations by which in Nature one thing passes away into another.

In a period when landscape planning was a burning topic, Wordsworth fancied (as no doubt half the squirearchy fancied themselves) that he had a natural talent as an artist in that direction. Rawnsley has collected the local recollections of him in his later years, as self-appointed arbiter of taste in every planting and felling, as well as in every alteration to any building. Since he lived to busy himself with this sort of thing to a ripe old age, we no doubt even to-day see the results of his intervention in detail, acting as a conservative force in this respect until the middle of the nineteenth century, far into a time concerned with other things.

CHAPTER XIII

MOTIONS AND MEANS

IN 1950 WAS CELEBRATED in the Lake District the centenary of the death of William Wordsworth, whose name is so often bracketed with that of the country itself. Special services were held in village churches, lectures were delivered by American professors, and tableaux were acted by schoolchildren. Bunches of daffodils, two fairly large and one very large, graced his resting-place at Grasmere, whilst the National Trust with ever-ready tact was at hand to suggest to motorcoach passengers how they might improve their minds and tastes by visits to the numerous associated shrines under its control. 80,000 people visited Dove Cottage during the year. Altogether, though without unbecoming ostentation or sensationalism, his countrymen, especially the self-adopted ones, decently remembered the countryside's greatest son.

It must be admitted that there is a very considerable discrepancy between the aims and outlook of the modern lovers of the Lake District and the aims and personality of Wordsworth. A great poet cannot even in retrospect be fitly harnessed to the tourist popularity of a particular district, apart from the fact that it might well have happened as a matter of history that he lived out his life in the Quantocks or North Dorset.

In his own lifetime, his residence in the Lake District was the cause of a few other select spirits residing there, and through a later period a substantial fraction of the visitors to the Lakes might have been seen, guide-book in hand, identifying the sources of his inspiration. One visualises this roughly between 1840 and 1900, which fits in well enough with the usual time-lag and cycle of fashion in such matters.

At the mention of Wordsworth's name, something like a

lion is seen to be standing in our road. The beast does not typify the poet himself, but rather symbolises vested critical interests and the formidable questions raised by his philosophy, questions we are glad to sidetrack and leave to better-equipped critics. But it is doubtful if either reader or author can honestly do so entirely. Our business in not with philosophy except so far as it enters into our corner of social history. But Wordsworth himself covers the whole range between subtle philosophical argument and the most pedestrian observation. Some have thought the gap too wide:

> Two voices are there. One is of the deep;
> The other of an old and silly sheep. . . .

As a factor in the tourist popularity of the district, his effect can easily be overestimated, but his statements of the essential reasons which lead us there challenge all of us. In their pure form, they stand on the record. But when we come to consider his life, so deliberately identified with his philosophy on the one hand and with the rocks and streams of our district on the other, we have to ask ourselves whether anything so complicated as even the simplest human being—especially one of pre-eminent sensibility—can be so simply accounted for. And, if any doubts suggest themselves, in the case of one who so much lived by the book, it must be on the philosophy that they reflect.

It is not, after all, the special business of a poet to live his own principles. We should be grateful to him for the vagrant lights his poetry gives us, whether he lived up to its social and other implications or not. We cannot all, in addition to producing ideologically correct poetry, be Stakhanovites and devoted fighters on the barricades as well. Many poets failed to try at all, whilst some of those who have worked out in their lives ideas which have in later times been much admired in their literary dress were least appreciated by those who personally knew them best. It is just the close apparent correspondence between Wordsworth's writings and doings in the long afternoon and evening of his life that gives interest to the question what exactly they both amounted to.

The charge has been brought against him of admitting into his life a self-betrayal, in regard to his early political views, occasioned perhaps by his unhappy love-affair, which caused him to renounce first the cause of revolutionary France, then that of liberty, then even of humanity—with the result that poetry in turn deserted him. In truth, what is known of the facts will easily allow of other explanations, such as the excesses of the French, or the ordinary effects of middle age; although this may simply be saying the same thing in an attenuated way. And did he desert the greater for the less, or vice-versa? If, in meditation on nature, we look through nature up to nature's God, the world may be well lost. Even the allegedly formal and prosaic eighteenth century did not have to wait for Wordsworth to discover this. And Wordsworth himself did not always fly quite so high as this. The transports of self-forgetfulness in the contemplation of natural order, whether exampled in some tiny flower or crystal or in the more abstract consideration of its place in the scheme of things, is surely a more deeply poetical occupation than, let us say, the exercise of taste in landscape arrangement, which one might well call a sort of outdoor trade of upholstery. If communion with nature has a supreme value, then clearly it cannot be necessary to insist on its taking place only amid the beautiful scenery of any particular district, nor possible to deny that the simple life may be effectually cultivated in a wide variety of places, whether in striking scenery or not. The inducements to which he appeals in his letters to the papers against the Windermere railway, viz: 'Schemes of retirement sown in youth' and 'the degree of attachment which many of the yeomanry feel to their small inheritances' cannot be for everyone. The undue taste for 'far-winding valleys difficult of access' is from a psychiatric point of view even a little suspect in itself. Yet such things are picturesque indeed and are subjects for poetry, though not in the highest degree.

Wordsworth's achievement (leaving aside all but a few of his poems) was in the descent from greater arguments and passions to carefully regulated smaller ones, and the painstaking reconstruction of happiness by the practice of an applied art of living, using the simplest material.

The two accounts of the Lakes scenery and its impact, which no one can afford not to read every word of, are Gray's too-brief *Journal*, and, for altogether later mental weather, Wordsworth's *Description of the Scenery* (which in a later edition bore the title of '*Guide*' etc.). This not only became popular, but was well thought of by the poet himself; and he continued revising it from its first appearance in 1810, until 1835, the latest edition to be produced in his own lifetime. If he sometimes versified very prosily, he seldom wrote anything in either verse or prose without sound sense, delicate reflectiveness and the limpidity of style that comes of taking pains. A work of this sort was not at all beneath him: he considered his native aptitudes fitted him for three professions —poet, landscape gardener, and critic of pictures and works of art. The triply-divided ambition sheds light on the spirit in which he attacked each task separately. He begins by surveying the early picturesque explorers:

A practice, denominated Ornamental Gardening, was . . . becoming prevalent over England. In union with an admiration of this art, and in some cases in opposition to it, had been generated a relish for select parts of natural scenery; and Travellers, instead of confining their observations to Towns, Manufactories, or Mines began (a thing till then unheard of) to wander over the island in search of sequestered spots, distinguished as they might accidently have learned, for the sublimity or beauty of the forms of Nature there to be seen. Dr Brown, the celebrated Author, etc. . . .

This historical exordium is characteristic of Wordsworth's whole attitude, and has its counterpart in the deep and objective respect with which he approaches natural features great and little, to penetrate to their true understanding before permitting himself flights of subjective enthusiasm. Historical awareness is often stated to be part of the

Romantic Movement in general, but it plays a very different part in his case from the case of Walter Scott, who was apt to look for the atmospheric effects first and the actual local colour afterwards. From this respect for essential character derive Wordsworth's ideas on Planning: 'The rule is simple. Work, where you can, in a spirit of Nature, with an invisible hand of art.' (He is here speaking in particular of the grounds of a mansion; *a fortiori* of wilder scenes.) These views, however, we will not take space to develop here, as they are worth studying at length in the original.

Towards the end of Wordsworth's long evening, in 1844, he addressed two letters to the *Morning Post* on the proposed branch railway from Kendal to Windermere, which was constructed, in spite of his protest, a few years after. In the first letter he discusses the faculty for appreciating beauty. He again appeals to history, to prove that:

'A vivid perception of romantic scenery is neither inherent in mankind nor a necessary consequence of even a comprehensive education.' 'Green fields, clear blue skies . . . and all the ordinary varieties of rural nature . . . find an easy way to the affections of all men . . . but a taste beyond this is not to be implanted at once.' 'Rocks and mountains, torrents and wide spread waters . . . cannot, in their finer relations to the human mind, be comprehended, or can be very imperfectly conceived, without processes or opportunities of culture in some degree habitual.'

It was therefore of no benefit to bring excursionists wholesale to the Lake scenery. 'Let us rather look with lively sympathy' (he remarks in a tone which in anyone else one would think a little supercilious) 'upon persons in that condition' (that is, artisans, labourers, and the humbler classes of shopkeepers) 'when, upon a holiday, or on the Sunday, after having attended divine worship, they make little excursions with wives and children among the neighbouring fields' (those, let us suppose, near their slum homes in newly-built Ancoats). He then goes on to treat Robert Burns to a page or two of patronising commiseration for reacting only to daisies, field-mice and such, and not to the scenes most approved by a

purified and developed taste for ornamental gardening.
How would the boy of Hawkshead School half a century
earlier have felt about this? It is not possible, on the evidence
of these letters, to acquit Wordsworth of being somewhat
lacking in sympathy for humanity, even for that minority
who might be inherently capable of learning to share his own
tastes. Yet, as he defends himself in the second letter, against
the not unnatural charge of indifference to the enjoyment of
the poor, we get a little more insight into his motives. The
real adversary, perhaps, was not the humble excursionists,
but utilitarianism, and those who sheltered behind its
name, such as the greedy company promoters of the railway
decade, whose activities he would scarcely have thought any
more tolerable in London than at Windermere; and his
opposition to the railway was but a shot in a wider, and
nobler, battle. With the whole vista of nineteenth- and
twentieth-century industrial expansionism to look back on,
with its world-wide consequences, down to the atomic age,
we may feel not quite certain about his being on the wrong
side. At least he was fairly consistent.

It is strange to reflect that, although we owe to him the
expression 'National Park' (or rather, in his own words,
'National Property') he would, wrongly or rightly, have
failed to be a wholehearted adherent of the National Park
movement to-day. Can we suppose, for example, that he
would have been sympathetic to week-end motoring or
cycling, rushed visits to the mountains merely for the sake of
variety and exercise and as a makeweight to a very different
existence elsewhere, but without even the wish to subordinate mind and heart to the influences of simplicity and
natural objects? Would he have been rejoiced by the raucous
shouts of climbers, sounding as if through a megaphone,
from rocky gullies? If there is any conflict of interest between
ramblers and farmers, which side would he have been on?
No one who reads even these two letters, and the *Description*,
can be in doubt. I do not attempt to mediate here, but merely
recall that Wordsworth's wider human sympathies have

already been called in question. Yet, consider the application of the following sonnet, composed 'some years before 1837' and re-promulgated in 1844, to the modern questions of reservoirs and of transmission lines for electricity, and of the other physical necessities of modern civilisation:

STEAMBOATS AND RAILWAYS

Motions and means, on land and sea at war
with old poetic feeling, not for this
shall ye by poets even be judged amiss.
Nor shall your presence, howsoe'er it mar
the loveliness of nature, prove a bar
to the mind's gaining that prophetic sense
of future good, that point of vision, whence
may be discovered what in soul ye are;
In spite of all that beauty must disown
in your harsh features, nature doth embrace
her lawful offspring in man's art; and Time,
pleased with your triumphs o'er his brother Space,
accepts from your bold hand the proffered crown
of hope, and welcomes you with cheer sublime.

It is pretty plain that it was the promoters and the passengers that Wordsworth disliked, more than the propulsion, the pylons, or the permanent way, and this too at a time when industrial design was in its crude infancy.

CHAPTER XIV

THE SETTLERS

THE TOURIST who, from his enjoyment of his brief excursion in summer, made the rash inference that he would find equal satisfaction in living always at the Lakes, had to consider how best he could reconcile the house he would have to build with the picturesque character of the country. To take the practical steps involved in house-building must very understandably be something of a responsibility in a landscape which had been associated with romantic, even fantastic, notions; where dreadful physical cataclysms were constantly felt to threaten, among scenes which the beholders repeatedly declared were productive of mystical experience, and said to be inhabited by brigands, simple children of nature, quaint characters such as the miserly King of Patterdale, and the 'poor naturals' who specially appealed to Wordsworth.

At the same time, if one is to enjoy any of that solid comfort upon which the higher appreciative faculties so palpably depend, a house one must have. Gilpin, whose mission it was above all to show people how to indulge romantic fancies practically, did not blink this. In the halcyon days of the rococo taste, it might be well enough for the disciples of Gray or of Horace Walpole to affect a taste for residing in grottoes or lightning-riven trees, but for the seventeen-eighties, post-chaises and turnpikes were making the problem an urgent and practical one.

So the house must be what it will, and the garden must be sacrificed. 'A house is an artificial object,' says Gilpin, 'and the scenery around it may be considered as the connecting thread between the regularity of the house and the freedom of the natural scene.' The garden should pass, by gradations as rapid as may be, to the inspired disorder of nature. Gilpin

with practised casuistry consoles himself, firstly for this
rather self-indulgent solution, by admitting that the
picturesque and the rational or 'moral' (as represented by
human industry) are irreconcilable. In the second place, he
says, it is really not possible anyhow to do any better in
practice. 'Indeed I question whether it were possible for a
single hand to build a picturesque village.' Finally, it will all
be for the best:

> On the spot, no doubt, and even in the first distance, the marks of the
> spade, and the plough, and the hedge, and square divisions of property,
> are disgusting (i.e. distasteful) in a high degree. But when all these
> regular forms are softened by distance—when hedgerow trees begin to
> unite, and lengthen into streaks along the horizon—when farmhouses
> and ordinary buildings lose their vulgarity of shape, and are scattered
> about in formless spots, through the several parts of a distance—it is
> inconceivable what richness and beauty this mass of deformity, when
> melted together, adds to a landscape.

The first man, so Wordsworth says, who ever settled in
the Lakes for the sake of the scenery was a Mr. English,
who came from Nottinghamshire. He was not troubled at
all by scruples of the kind Gilpin entertained. The architect
John Plaw built for him, between 1773 and 1778, the fine
circular house which still stands on Belle Isle, in its original
layout one of the most conspicuous sites to be found near
Windermere.* The whole island was planted, fruit-walls were
built, a formal garden laid out, and a path was made to
run round the shoreline. The aim was clearly to embellish
the landscape by providing it with a conspicuous and central feature, and as such the house was accepted by nearly
every artist who thereafter visited the Lakes, for 50 years,
for a glimpse of it appears in every set of prints. Could it be
pleaded that there was not necessarily anything inconsistent,
between appreciation of the view from the island, and of the
formal style of these improvements? The essential character
inherent in a landscape of so large a scale as that of Windermere could not really be affected by a little gardening?

---

* The plans of the house are contained in Plaw's *Rural Architecture* (1785)

Ridge still rose behind ridge, across the wide-spread lake. Villas on Italian Alpine lakes had also been formally planned. But house, plantation, wall and path were fiercely condemned by every subsequent writer on Lake District scenery, down to and including Wordsworth. 'A Dutch burgomaster's palace,' says Hutchinson. Overwhelmed, Mr. English sold the house before it was completed, and the purchaser, Miss Curwen, mitigated the effect by the abandonment of the offending wall and path, and by the re-planting of the island, so as to make a 'natural' (i.e. irregular) screen of trees. When this was done the scheme was generally admitted to be pardonable. Clarke says Hutchinson's onslaught was the sole reason for the change. The formal layout, originally adopted, had certainly been representative of the landscape ideas of the early eighteenth century rather than of the 'natural' style of Capability Brown, more recently popular. It was the way of the world that the stranger who gave to the district the most distinguished single effort of design it ever had should have to resign the fame of it to a local grandee of sufficient weight to overrule any mere aesthetic objection.

Although the battle of styles was once and for all decided at Belle Isle, yet building must have been very active from then onwards. In his 1796 edition Thomas West can record the following lately built houses in the neighbourhood of Windermere: Mr. Law's house at Brathay, Miss Pritchard's Croft Lodge, Mr. Harrison's above Ambleside, Mrs. Taylor's cottage at Ambleside, Bishop Watson's Calgarth (formerly an ancient farm), Mrs. Taylor's Belfield, Sir John Legerd's Storrs, Mr. Dixon's Fell Foot, Mr. Machels at Newby Bridge, Belmont at Esthwaite, and the Rev'd William Brathwaite's summerhouse on Claife Common. Also, Sir Michael le Fleming had recently made a new front to Rydal Hall, 'in a good style, which gives it a very interesting appearance'. It is not the old family mansions, like Rydal, or Dove Nest, which concern us here, unless by the accident of one or two of them being rebuilt at this time in the

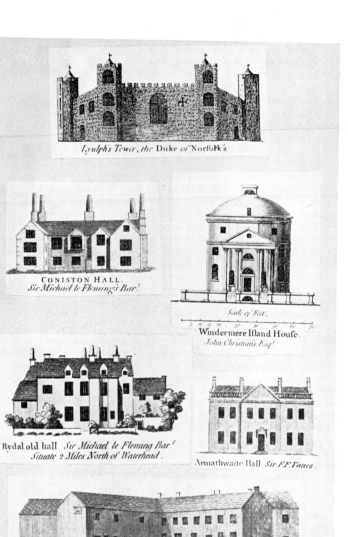

Lyulph's Tower, the Duke of Norfolk's

CONISTON HALL.
Sir Michael le Fleming's Bar.t

Scale of Feet.

Windermere Ifland Houfe.
John Christian's Esq.r

Rydal old hall Sir Michael le Fleming Bar.t
Situate 2 Miles North of Waterhead.

Armathwaite Hall Sir F.F.Vanes

Low-wood Inn Wright's

SIX WAYS OF LIVING IN THE LAKE DISTRICT

Rydal, since reconstructed, and Coniston are the
only pre-xviith century examples

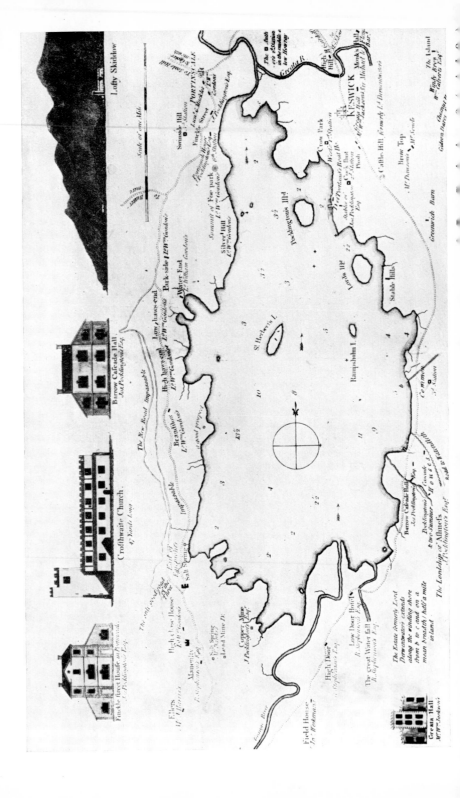

romantic spirit, and this the owners of them would be less likely to do than newcomers. It is not always easy to classify an individual definitely as one of these or the other. To the list given by West, who best knew the southern lakes, we may add other houses around Bassenthwaite, most of them more or less new, and mentioned by Clarke (1787) whose book dealt mainly with the northern side of the district. These were Ullock, where the last of the Earl of Derwentwater's family lived; Powterhow, 'a pretty building'; Wood End; the elegant new-built mansion of Thomas Storey at Mirehouse; Miss Curwen's cottage at Ousebridge; and Armathwaite, which West called 'The Queen of the Vale'. This was also a modern construction, but was mentioned by Gray, and was therefore rather too early to be other than in the Georgian style. It had a balustraded parapet, chimneys treated in a Georgian manner, an advanced centre wing, and the principal doorway seems to have been classical in treatment. There were also Lisick-Hall; Dyke Nook, 'a fanciful little cot'; and Dr. Brownrigg's Ormathwaite, which 'house and everything round it are planned in all the charming simplicity of refined taste'. The modern inn at Ousebridge had been built by Mr. Spedding, the owner of Armathwaite. Around Derwentwater the hand of Mr. Joseph Pocklington had been very active, in the house on Vicar's Island, at Barrow Hall, and at Finkle Street House (afterwards Derwent Bank) in Portinscale, all much alike and illustrated on Crosthwaite's Map (1783). Greta Hall, not mentioned by Clarke, was surmounted by a crenellation. Lord Lewis Gordon's Water End was unpretentious. The upper end of Ullswater seems to have been almost free from new mansions, as were the vale of Grasmere, and the actual villages of Ambleside and Bowness. The Lakes were colonised too late for anything else like the house on Belle Isle to be attempted, so that we are denied the interesting spectacle the country would have presented if during the earlier part of the eighteenth century ambitious newcomers had successively left the traces of their own taste in the remodelling of a landscape.

H

In his dislike of 'spottiness' and angularity, Gilpin's
precepts were in harmony with the ideas of most of his
contemporaries. But the prophets of this cult of nature varied
among themselves in the strictness of their doctrine. Far to
the left of Gilpin was Richard Payne Knight, the Herefordshire squire, who is still better known as a Greek archaeo-
logist. Knight was a more consistent thinker, and he
showered criticism on Gilpin, who was an easy mark for it,
as well as on the older-fashioned landscapists. In place of
Gilpin's scruples about the function of architecture in rural
surroundings, Knight was ready almost for abnegation of it.
So far from gardens being laid out with any reference to the
house, the house itself and its purlieus were to be sub-
ordinated to the natural landscape.

> So, let th'approach and entrance to your place
> Display no glitter, and affect no grace;
> But still in careless easy curves proceed
> Through the rough thicket and the flowery mead,
> Till, bursting from some deep imbowr'd shade,
> Some narrow valley, or some opening glade,
> Well mixed and blended in the scene, you shew
> The stately mansion rising to the view.
> But mixed and blended, ever let it be
> A mere component part of all you see.

A specimen ideal landscape from his own book shows a
mansion in a rhapsodic Tudor style which equally deserves
to be called 'horrid' in either the ancient or the modern
senses of that word. The grounds are, if anything, rather
wilder than nature. It is said that on his own estate he
experimented with foregrounds constructed by casting down
rough blocks of stone at random, and training brambles over
them.

Like most zealots, Knight is more antagonised by his own
schismatical co-religionists than by the heathen themselves.
He scorns the whole tribe of landscape gardeners, who had
'leaped the fence and saw all nature as a garden', and wishes
to shut them in again in their proper perspective. He is
particularly strong against serpentine paths, set views, and

expanses of lawn. He speaks thus of the Stuart manor houses,
such as Levens, of the days prior to landscape gardenings:

> Though the old system against nature stood,
> At least in this, 'twas negatively good:—
> Inclosed by walls, and terraces and mounds,
> Its mischiefs were confined to narrow bounds,
> They never dared invade the open grounds.

> . . . . . . Ye rural muses, weep
> The ivied balustrades, and terrace steep;
> walls, mellowed into harmony by time,
> O'er which fantastic creepers used to climb
> While statues, labyrinths, and alleys pent
> Within their bounds, at least were innocent.

As regards ruins, Gilpin in his preference upon the Gothic
style is sufficiently orthodox to escape Knight's direct
condemnation. 'It is not every man that can build a house,'
says Gilpin, 'who can execute a ruin. To give the stone its
mouldering appearance, to make the widening chink run
naturally through all the joints, to scatter heaps of ruin
around with negligence and ease, are great efforts of art.'
For the same reason he deplores the vandalism that would
restore ruins. In his insistence on structural knowledge and
honest workmanship (in the construction of ruins) and on
not doing violence to nature, as well as in his inconsistencies
and dogmatic tone, Gilpin curiously anticipates Ruskin.

Genuine Gothic ruins are welcomed warmly by Knight,
but where it is necessary to manufacture them 'English
Nature' must 'claim from art the appearance of neglect' and
'no decoration would we introduce, that has not first been
nat'ralised by use'.

> But let no servile copyist appear
> To plant his paltry imitations here
> And shew poor Baalbec dwindled to the eye
> And Paestum's fanes with columns six feet high
> With urns and cenotaphs our vallies fill
> And bristle o'er with obelisks the hill!

With respect to the subsidiary architectural ornaments of
a garden or a landscape, there had been recommended in

West's *Guide* (1778) '. . . a particular that would greatly contribute to the perfection of this beautiful region, to have proper objects placed on some of the eminences with which it abounds'.

These, the author of the *Ode* (1780) suggests, should take the form of

neat inscribed pillars, tablets etc. by the affluent visitors, near a favourite lake or station, commemorative of some friend, person of genius, etc. or of the time when they themselves enjoyed the pleasure of viewing the surrounding objects. They might thus, in a part which gives the fairest play to genuine feeling and fancy, either evince their regard for merit and their love of nature, or record their friendships, and recall to the minds of posterity, that they too had visited Arcadia. The undertaking would not only beautify these scenes, and give occasion to many a pleasing reflection, but, I flatter myself, be a credit to the national taste, and in time become itself a new inducement to make a tour. . . .

This is quite in harmony with the Hutchinsonian senti-ment, and the same views continued through several successive eras of taste. Not every amateur of landscape belonged to the puritan school of Payne Knight, which would have disapproved, but it is very likely the early settlers in the Lakes were further advanced towards Knight's views than most people—had it not been so, they would not have migrated thither.

Architectural landscape ornament falls for our purposes into three or four classes. Earliest in origin was the Italian school of garden design, which preceded the Dutch, and consisted, in Repton's words, in 'ballustraded terraces of masonry, magnificent flights of steps, arcades, and archi-tectural grottoes, lofty clipped hedges, with niches and recesses enriched by sculpture'. Nothing of this sort ever formerly existed in the Lakes although the style much in favour in the local designs of the early twentieth century is very reminiscent of it. This style, which (with its suggestion of domestic life in the open air) the eighteenth century at length reluctantly admitted to be unsuited to the English climate, was at length only echoed in such half-regretful

POCKLINGTON'S ISLAND, DERWENTWATER

by T. Otway, 1783

POCKLINGTON'S ISLAND.

Done to Lieut. Col.ⁿ Wm Peachy in the Year 1796.

The Battery 43 feet — 2

N Druid's Stone 6.8 high — 6

The Boat House 16 feet — 3

Length of the Island 1.3.5.0

Breadth 1.69 1.5.5

The Fort 33 feet long — 4

Saint Mary's Church 25 feet high — 7

The House on the Center of the Island — 5

Druid Temple 36 feet diameter

POCKLINGTON'S PASTICHES

suggestions as the footnote above-quoted from the *Ode*. The statues which, in accordance with this taste, used to grace the grounds of Holker Hall, near Cartmel, were removed in the first years of the nineteenth century. Statues like these had a hard fate. Buried and neglected in their native Italy (although sometimes not nearly so long buried as their English purchasers supposed), they were reft from it only to be exposed, often quite insufficiently clothed, to the rheumaticky damps of an English garden, and finally banished, who knows where, perhaps, in fragments, to a rock garden in the suburbs of Barrow-in-Furness.

It was this style, drawing its symbols from literary sources, with no concession to the particular landscape to which it was applied, to which Knight objected. It was an expression of the view that nature was only a text for man to expatiate upon in whatever way and to what extent he pleased, not a living teacher whose disciple he should be.

Generally, the prevailing tone in this manner of decorating a garden was one of literary allusion, and gentle melancholy, reminiscent of the classics. But sometimes the more robust play-instinct came uppermost. A Mr. Joseph Pocklington, who came from Nottinghamshire, put up a number of buildings on Vicar's Island in Derwentwater, which he purchased in 1778. They were not at all what they appeared to be, and ranged from a bogus druidical circle to a make-believe church and a couple of sham forts. This was generally felt to be not quite playing the game. His *lusi naturae* (so to call them) are shown on Peter Crosthwaite's map of 1783, but were gone, or remodelled, by the time of Green's *Guide*. The main dwelling-house on the island was in a Georgian style.

The third style was that of Gilpin and his ruins, which we have already mentioned, together with other Gothick trifles. This was fairly well represented in the Lakes. There was the ruin on the island off Conishead Priory, the 'Station' at the west side of Windermere Ferry, Mr. King's summer-house on the hill-top at Finsthwaite, near Newby Bridge, and the structure on the hill above Lindal, visible from the main road. One of the last 'Gothick' ruins was that in front of Wray Castle, which was erected after the middle of the 19th century. A 'Hermitage' with thatched roof, portico of rough tree trunks, and windows of 'Gothick' shape, was put up about 1800 by Sir Wilfrid Lawson on St. Herbert's Isle in Derwentwater. The legend of this sixth-century saint was very dear to our great-great-grandfathers, of the age when 'hermits' were sometimes employed by landscape dilettanti to dwell in grottoes on their estates. If St. Herbert had not lived in such an ideal situation, it would surely have been necessary to invent him.

A fourth and last style was that of the return to classicism. Once again mankind, in spite of Green and Payne Knight, made bold to assert their presence in the landscape. Everywhere in the country, except in the Lakes, the battles of Trafalgar and Waterloo and the officers who took part in them, were commemorated by obelisks high on hill tops, pylons, Grecian columns, and masonry of an Egyptian massiveness—memorials making their appeal not to the old-fashioned allusive melancholy, but to national or family pride. At first glance, one might think the sites and opportunities for this sort of thing abounded in Cumbria. We can only suppose, everything considered, that sheer sense of fitness forbade it. A comparatively inoffensive little example was Sir John Legerd's classical Temple of the Heroes, at Storrs, dedicated to Lords Howe, St. Vincent, Duncan of Camperdown, and Nelson. It was furnished with an organ. Christopher North wrote a poem on it in all good faith: the Stranger, he says, was not to smile at its venturing to stand, a plaything of art, amid the great forms of nature, in defiance of the highest (i.e. picturesque) rules of grace. No cold unmeaning outrage was meant to nature's sanctity, but the bold peasantry were to be reminded by it of the nation's maritime glory, and so on.

But to return to the subject of dwellinghouses. It was the 'Gothick' style which, of the four we have mentioned, was most closely associated, both by date and, as was thought, by inherent fitness, with Lake District scenery. As regards dwelling-houses, the earliest Gothick effort was Lyulph's Tower, on Ullswater, on the Duke of Norfolk's estates. It was built prior to 1783. It expresses the exuberant sensationalism of the early romantics, up to Gilpin. For, whilst intended to look like the fortress of a robber baron, it was really hardly more than a gamekeeper's cottage, with low ceilings and tiled floors. Budworth was told that the Duke, when residing there, would use no chairs, but only benches, with 'a long hospitable board' for a table—much as Mr. Chainmail did in *Crotchet Castle*. The later, more dogmatic romantics succeeded in persuading themselves that, whilst shams were highly immoral, such Gothic edifices were not really shams, but natural developments fitting to the landscape in which they stood.

The attempt of the romantic period to devise architecture for dwelling-houses on the principles of nature, therefore, began by the reproduction, often inharmonious and exotic, of particular kinds of buildings (principally Gothic castles) which in themselves evoked romantic sentiments. It then passed through the stage where any sort of style at all was regarded with suspicion, and interest centred in accidental circumstances, the appearance of age, unobtrusiveness and so on. The dates when these and subsequent ideas respectively came first into fashion among cognoscenti can be fairly closely defined, but the periods during which they were actually put into practice are naturally harder to fix. Everyone who happened to be building contemporarily with Knight's writings had not necessarily arrived at the same development of ideas.

The old halls, farm-houses, and cottages of the North of England, says Green in 1817, 'have long been admired for their elegant peculiarity of design'. At first sight it is a little surprising, since the imitation of the smaller Gothic type of building did not come about for many years. Ever since Horace Walpole had in 1747 put up Strawberry Hill, at

Twickenham, it had not been uncommon to build small residences like Lyulph's Tower, even down to summer-houses, as if they were merely miniatures of the great mediaeval fortresses or abbeys. But Green may possibly be referring to a feeling of local people of instinctive taste for the native style to which they were accustomed. Most probably, however, he is not really referring to any definite and characteristic local features, but to the simple 'picturesqueness' of ancient structures, the product of time and accident; to the moss on the roof, rather than to the structural features. As Green said, the local style 'recommends itself most when aided by accidental additions and dilapidations, and by combinations of the richest woods and backgrounds'. The picturesque school was, when Green wrote, many years old, but exact observation of the real characteristics of the more modest types of ancient structures was only just beginning. Green's own careful draughtsman-ship must indeed have done much to support a fondness for the real Lakeland style.

In the opinion of the picturesque school, the colour of houses was likewise governed principally, and the site itself to a great extent, by the same principle of inconspicuousness. White as a colour for a building offended against this principle, but it was nevertheless popular with the general public. White houses, it was said, broke up the view into triangles: it was not remembered that the dot of white might have the same effect in a landscape as the man in bright red or blue jacket so frequently introduced by landscape painters of the period, and with such happy effect. Houses of the local slate were rough-cast as a matter of course and Green complained of much 'paring and plastering' of old buildings. Wordsworth endorsed Sir Joshua Reynolds' dictum that anyone who wished to know the proper colour for his house should 'turn up a stone, or pluck a handful of grass by the roots, and see what is the colour of the soil where the house is to stand'. He had to admit exceptions to this rule, where the soil was very dark or, as in the Cumbrian coastal regions, bright red. The safest colour, he considered, was something between cream and a dust colour, commonly called a stone colour. (This sounds suspiciously like the dreary ochreous or slaty hues of Victorian stucco.) By 1835, he could, in a footnote, report that 'a proper colouring for houses is now becoming universal'.

The real objection was to any reminder at all of the presence of man in a landscape. Nowadays we have given up the battle as lost, where lowland and wooded landscapes are concerned. Houses were then recommended to be surrounded by trees, not so much for shelter as to protect the romantically-minded passer-by from seeing any evidence of habitation.*

By the first decade of the nineteenth century, although, as we have said, it was the greater castles and abbeys which had first struck the romantic imagination, local antiquarians like the Revd. Mr. Hodgson were beginning to observe and describe in detail the characteristic features of the fortified manor houses and ancient farms of the north. (Sir Hugh Walpole reproduced, verbatim, in his novel *Rogue Herries*, Hodgson's description of the ancient Westmorland farmhouse.) But it is not recorded that anyone, in building a new house of modest size, attempted reproduction or even a development of any of these genuinely ancient ones. Instead, when Green wrote, what was called the 'Modern Gothic' was in full popularity. It was admitted that this was a style which had never been used in the Middle Ages, but it was considered to be compounded of the mediaeval 'Church Gothic' and 'Castle Gothic'.

In Sir George Knott's house at Coniston Waterhead, built before the nineteenth century (and thus an early example of its kind)

the pointed arched windows on the projecting front, and the elegant crosses on the gables, are strictly Church, while the label mouldings on the square windows, and the square bastions with turrets and portices

* But by 1820, says Briggs, a reaction had already begun against this 'hiding away houses in the corners of fields'.

incline to the Castle Gothic. A medium, however, has been nicely observed. The buttress and pinnacle of the sacred architecture, and the watchtower and triple corbel of the military architecture are all avoided.

Inside the walls were executed in fresco, in imitation of wainscot. The chaste promiscuity of this was rivalled by its contemporary Conishead Priory 'which it is expected (1793) in a few years will be one of the most splendid buildings in the North of England'. 'The north front is in the Gothic style; this, and a piazza supported by clustered Gothic pillars, and three series of ox-eye windows, crowned with a battlement, give to the whole an elegant and respectable appearance.' Another structure in this taste (Holker Hall) 'approaches perhaps most nearly to the twelfth century, but considerably softened and mellowed by the light and lofty elegance of the present day.'

The extremes of the Gothic style were generally reserved for two classes of buildings—the greater seats of which something striking was expected, or the little jeux d'esprit such as summerhouses. But a style not widely different from the early Georgian was quite common, and is often simply called 'the modern style'. Though its looks are not much admired, it is usually expressed by such kindly-meant stock phrases as 'rather for convenience than display' or 'comfort is studied more than ostentation'. It is interesting to notice just what is incidentally covered by such a phrase about comfort, which is used for example in the case of Lunefield, a house near Lancaster built in 1815, and another of similar design at Cark: 'Mr. Newby's certainly excels in having all the kitchens completely underground. . . . Placing them underground, though perhaps not so agreeable to the inmates, is decidedly most pleasing to the eye of taste.' The style of house usually indicated by phrases such as these, often looked forward towards the neo-Gothic style by having projecting eaves, and backwards towards the Georgian by the pillars and entablature, and its air of foursquare upright symmetry. Bigger windows were a modern improvement.

It is rather easier to point to conspicuous examples of

particular styles in the open country upon its borders, where
lay the richest estates, than in the Lake District itself. Indeed,
eccentricity is lacking just where one might expect it. It was
on the borders of the area that were situated Lowther Castle
begun in 1802, and the other examples above quoted, except
Coniston Waterhead. 'Most of the Lake Villas (we are told
in 1822) are built rather for comfort than ostentatious
display.' The Croft, near Ambleside, is, however, in this
Gothick style (but with an impressive display of Tudor
chimneys). There is a little more latitude in cottages, that is
to say, gate lodges, and the cottage ornée, or rich man's
cottage. 'Projecting eaves, windows with iron mullions,
lozenge chimneys, and verandahs, are all that can be
admitted into Gothic cottage architecture.' If the builders
of workaday moderate-sized houses built at all in any style
which, by a stretch, could be called Gothic, it was in the
local style of their own fathers and grandfathers rather than
in the supposed 'Castle Gothic', or even the genuine farmhouse Gothic of the middle ages. Nearly all the larger houses
whose elevations are shown in the borders of Crosthwaite's
maps and of which most indeed were only erected since the
Lakes became known to sightseers, are frankly Georgian.

It does indeed seem that, early in the nineteenth century,
there was a strong reaction towards plainness, utility and
even baldness. The fact that more of all sorts of people were
building here helps to account for this. The increase in
favour of the genuine local style was, therefore, a healthy
as well as an inevitable development. Why, asks Wordsworth in the 1835 edition of his *Guide*

should the genius that directed the ancient architecture of these vales
have deserted them? For the bridges, churches, mansions, cottages and
their richly-fringed and flat roofed outhouses . . . have been substituted
structures in which baldness only seems to have been studied, or plans
of the most vulgar utility. But some improvement may be looked for in
future; the gentry *recently* have copied the old models.

Of course we should like to think that Wordsworth had
in view in the phrase 'the old models' only those genuine

old models which we approve to-day. He did not possess, and (considering his idiosyncratic temper) rather despised, too close an academic acquaintance with detail, except in so far as it might arise from his own casual personal observation. On the other hand, the more modern styles which Wordsworth condemned as harsh and utilitarian, may quite easily be the very ones with which for us nowadays are associated the thoughts of old-fashioned leisure and dignity; the unpretentious country house with its well-grouped windows (perhaps even its verandah), its lawn, and its park-fence—all its details a marriage of quiet convenience and taste. Very often, in Lakeland particularly, but also elsewhere, these were long and low rather than the box-shape of mid-Victorian times. Even the workhouses in many parts of England, of which so many were put up just a little later, seem to have been unable to escape altogether the prevailing good taste.

The moral of all this seems to be that nothing wears so well as utilitarianism, and as a matter of fact the eccentric-picturesque school, when speaking of structures already old in their own time, were the very people to point out this truth.

LOWTHER CASTLE

A fine example of Regency Baronial architecture (now in course of demolition)

WRAY CASTLE, WINDERMERE

Mid XIX century

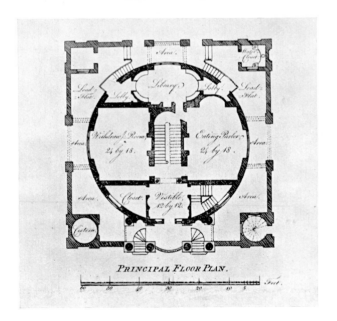

THE HOUSE ON BELLE ISLE
Internal arrangements

The circular house was surrounded by a square sunken area

CHAPTER XV

BANQUET ON OLYMPUS

'IT IS PROBABLE that no stranger ever sees that pier of Storrs without thinking of Professor Wilson. . . .' Thus wrote Harriet Martineau, seventeen years his junior.

. . . Anywhere, such a presence is rarely seen, and it was especially impressive in the places he best loved to haunt. More than one person has said that Wilson reminded them of the first man, Adam; so full was his large frame of vitality, force, and sentience. His tread seemed to shake the ground, and his glance to pierce through stone walls; and, as for his voice, there was no heart that could stand before it. In his hour of emotion, he swept away all hearts, whithersoever he would. . . . He made others happy by being so intensely happy himself, when his brighter moods were on him; and when he was mournful, no one desired to be gay.

John Wilson, or 'Christopher North', was contemporary as a Lake District resident with Green and Wordsworth (though in age a little younger than they) but he stands for a distinctly later development of the mode of enjoying the country. In some ways he brings the process to its culmination. He settled here to enjoy the converse of the poets, and, with equal gusto, all that the country afforded of general social life and especially sport. Of course he had another life —an Edinburgh-based one—as reviewer and descriptive writer, and the same gusto, the same irresponsibility (if that is not too mean a way to describe a rich and many-sided nature) is noticeable there too. As a writer, no one is more forthcoming and more inconsequent, gives more of himself or (of course within the limits of his own not small talents) lives more fully. Here is a man who has so much vitality that he has no need to prune and select his words and polish his sentences in order to make people listen to him.

He scatters gems of poetic feeling among heaps of careless verbiage, but one can never miss seeing that it was his living that was his art, and his writing only a by-product. Most critics cannot restrain themselves from cataloguing his imperfections, his downright faults, as a writer, but Christopher made them a free present of such opportunities. This generous spirit gave the British mountains a very high place in his affections.

We have never been able to sympathise with the luxury of that almost swooning sickness that assails the stranger in Switzerland, some ten or twelve thousand feet up the side of Mont Blanc, as the greedy guides drag the sumph along, sinking knee deep in the snow. Commend us, who are less ambitious, to a green grassy English mountain, or a purple heathery Scotch one, of such moderate dimensions as thine—O Coniston Old Man! There is some snow, like soap on thy beard; but thy chin is a Christian chin—and that cove is a pretty little dimple, which gives sweetness to thy smile. Strong are we on this summit as a stag—ay, we are indeed a hearty old Buck, and there goes our crutch like a rocket into the sky. Maga and the Old Man for ever!—hurra! hurra! hurra!

It is not easy to quote concisely for the purpose of illustrating the characteristic of discursiveness as such—the above-quoted passage is all I shall attempt, in order to introduce Christopher. It was he who (almost the first among fully articulate people), in all senses made the British mountains his own, driving body and temperament in double harness. It is not that he 'conquered' them physically, although many of his feats were then new. He bathed in nearly every stream and lake. He took his horses from Wasdale to Langdale by Esk Hause. He made many long hikes. He learned from the shepherds the scrambling route up Broad Stand and ascended Scafell from practically every direction. He swapped lies with Ritson of Wasdale. It is for all this that one's heart goes out to him. He can turn, so wholeheartedly that the abruptness seems not in the least to matter, from discussion of man's place in nature to the praises of eating, and from this he can abandon himself to the romantic spells of moonlight and pass slyly on to some practical joke such as a companion's being pushed into a river—almost as if he had himself pushed his reader into the

water. He welcomed any and every experience the country
could suggest, athletic, aesthetic, or contemplative.

In sequestered Duddondale, reading aloud from Wordsworth, and no doubt surrounded by the remains of an
excellent hamper lunch, he exclaims:

And what better might we do, lying here, all four of us, carelessly
diffused on the greensward far from the noisy world? . . . This is the way
to know and feel the spirit of this lovely and lonely, this barren and
beauteous land, where desolation lies in the close neighbourhood of
plenty, and where the hermit might find a secret cell within hearing of
the glad hum of life.

Each of these: desolation, plenty, contemplation, bustle,
eating, rejoicing, arduous physical effort, visual beauty,
abstract thought, the music or the power of words, he
knew how to savour, had life been long enough for all;
but to savour them most keenly one must drink of all by
turns.

By the side of Wilson, Wordsworth appears a myope,
Gilpin a self-deceiving pedant, Gray only a dabbler in mere
phantasies he was too idle to seek to relate to reality. By
comparison with Wilson's natural feeling and eloquence,
Ruskin's is the rhetoric of the sophist; in it, one is continually
apprehending, with a vague discomfort, the approach of the
too familiar cadence.

In Wilson the two worlds meet at last, that of the peasant,
the real mode of whose life was ignored by the polite world,
and the literates, who, so often, in the rhetorical mode of
the early eighteenth century, had undervalued the objective
approach. Let us go to see, said Samuel Johnson, sufficient
for the contemplation of a philosopher. But how much of the
piquancy for us of Johnson's own conversation (though for
his contemporaries it might be a different matter) depends
on the grotesque interaction of his scholarly polish and his
rough provincial sense!

For some of this, credit is not exclusively due to John
Wilson, for he had predecessors. There was, for instance,

the sturdy Wilkinson of Yanwath near Penrith, a local farmer of some education, and friend of William and Dorothy, who had the real modern sentiment for mountains as individuals, the peak-bagging spirit. A Quaker, he always seemed to get the best of both worlds, sitting down to breakfast with the Duke of Argyll's party at Campbeltown by no conscious deception of his own, just a matter of mutual mistake. He seems to have had remarkable luck on many of his climbs in Lakeland, in having the company of several very active young ladies, who are recorded as scrambling on ahead and appearing on dizzy ledges above. His book, *Tours to the British Mountains*, which appeared in 1824, covers more than one preceding decade.

Wilson was thus in a special position to assess the human meaning of the contact of man and nature. He, in fact, several times comes near to dealing with certain subjects which still, to-day as much as ever, exercise many people's minds: What is man's relation to the bit of the earth he knows, to what he calls 'nature'—its apparent beauty, its apparent cruelty or indifference—its sublime scale of size and power—its invitations to enjoyment, to exertion, to transcendental knowledge, to mystical union. One does not speak of man as scientist, as metaphysician, as expositor of any extrinsic dogma, or even perhaps in his specialised function as poet; one does not speak of the earth as the astronomer or as the geographer or engineer sees it, nor of any abstract 'earth', but of the spiritual relation of Everyman to the complex of stones, trees, winds, mountain-shapes, which he sees and feels. 'Insensate Seathwaite, what art thou but an assemblage of rocks, stones, clods, clumps and trees? Our imagination it was that vivified thee with beauty—till thou becamest symbolical of all spiritual essences, embodied poetry of a paradisiacal state of being.'

We cannot spare time to probe all the implications of the problem, but here we have, for what it is worth, Christopher's version of a subject so many writers about mountains have found it necessary to deal with:

The chasm is a dismal prison in which Stanley Ghyll Force,* like a madman, is raging with his chains. Dismal! Why that sunburst has changed the gloom into glory, and the Force is joyful as a bridegroom on his wedding day. How got the wild flowers up yonder among the mosses and the lichens, and how dare they smile so among the loose-hanging ledges of the rocks? God and God only, knows. The dreadful grows the beautiful, there is no anger in the torrent's voice in the very thunder there is love. The cauldron breathes up its mist to freshen the face of the precipice, and in the sparkling moisture the green'd trees rejoice. Gazing down the chasm thus filled, you find . . . a profusion of the loveliest things in nature, where you had expected to find, and at first had seen, but savage stern-ness and sterility.

'The dreadful grows the beautiful,' says Christopher, just as Frank Smythe also found. 'The brightest flowers grow on the borderland of death.'

One expects at this point the objection that one should go to philosophers for one's philosophy, and not to people like Wilson or Smythe, whose aim was first to disport them-selves in overcoming physical difficulties and then in the second place to entertain their readers. But perhaps the ordinary man's philosophy is underrated and the specialist's as in so many departments of life overrated. The feeling of the earth, filtering through the senses and the complex faculties of man's mind, which outrun logic, is a solid basis for philosophy, and more vivid and authentic to just those people who are least pre-occupied with systematic reasoning. Wilson reached perhaps as full a compromise as we ever see. These things are necessarily Everyman's business, and that is no doubt one reason why so many people who from one point of view have so little technical equipment for their task seem impelled to discourse on the notions—mental, metaphysical or mystical—suggested to them by their absorbing pastime of mountain climbing. Amongst all the roughage, husks and refuse of the natural unsorted product of sensation there may happen to be (in fact, is certain to be always) some indispensable vitamin which eludes those who succeed in refining the substance most delicately.

* Waterfall.

I

With all Wilson's boundless appetite for the arduous open air life about Wasdale or Glen Etive, and in spite of his linking mountain nature to poetry as a practical faith, he stops short deliberately of any vague worship of nature itself, and also refuses to regard the sublimity of nature or his own likings as in themselves principal arguments for religion. He certainly looks enquiringly in the direction of such a solution. 'Feeling, Taste, Genius, Virtue, Religion. Are they cognate only as all spiritual states are so, or are they sib . . . who shall expound the laws of all these holy things?' In another passage the mountain clouds tempt him to argue the same way (but he rejects their invitation after all):

Celestial ocean: shall our spirit, when our body dies, voyage on thee to the Eternal Shores? Yet what art thou, but a fair 'Congregation of Vapours' what hath the imagery of time to do with eternity! 'Tis but the mockery of Imagination after all—at the best symbolical—of thoughts that have their own independent being in the soul which is their birth place. The Faith that seems mighty to some, in one gazing, like us now, far and wide, and high and deep, on the splendours of this magnificent creation, till from the transient it soars into the transcendental, alas! how it languishes, grows dim and dies (when the observer is himself dying) knowing then that Faith is of diviner origin than Fancy—that the conscience which is in a man is awful, and cares nothing, at that hour, for the Beauty of the Clouds.

CHAPTER XVI

THE AGE OF SNOBS AND THE
AGE OF STEAM

MAN'S QUEST of natural living and natural beauty
neither begins nor ends with Christopher North,
although he almost completes its development. In
Blackwood's Magazine in 1832-3 Christopher published most of
what I have quoted, but he is referring back to a period of his
life much nearer to his own settling at Elleray by Windermere
in 1808. For a long while after Wilson's time, mute inglorious
Grays and Gilpins continued, as they always will, to re-
discover the sensation and reflection one can extract from
landscape. Every change in social history must bring its
characteristic shade of difference to the pastime of seeing
mountains. But of course it is less likely to be the first-rate
people of each period who will be concerned with a pastime,
once precedents and a routine have been established. From
the end of the Napoleonic wars the enterprising increasingly
sought their 'discoveries' in more distant regions; at the
least in the Highlands of Scotland, like Charles St John in
quest simply of sport, or the Sobieski Stuarts in search of a
romantic background; or in the Levant, like Byron, and
Kinglake, or like many a missionary or trader in far more
arduous journeys than any of these.

As time goes on, and fundamental impulses fade, social and
economic influences upon the fashion become more prominent. Here, for instance, is a day tripper of 1820 on Windermere, duly feeling what he ought to feel, after the best
models. There is something in his fluent eloquence which
puts one in mind of Dickens' Mr. Chadband:

> The dashing of the oars, softened by their distance, and the alternate
> blasts of a shrill-toned trumpet, mingling occasionally into a wild
> harmony, had something of a soothing influence in them, which cor-

responded with the prevailing taste of our minds. . . . We landed at the
Ferry Inn and advanced to the Station. We soon arrived at a superb
gate and entrance, set, as I thought, in mock majesty, at the foot of an
inaccessible rock and wood impervious. . . . The station building was
decorated with coloured glass of different hues—the effect of the scene,
when viewed through these, was such as the finest imagination might
perhaps in some propitious moment produce. . . . I could tell you how
the opposing mountains stretched along the side of the lake and how
delightfully Art had diversified it with groves and meadows. But I could
not tell you my feelings . . . how I stood some time mute with stupe-
faction. I could not tell you how a glow of admiration succeeded, and
how it operated in my breast, when motion returned to my frame, and
their wonted powers to the faculties. I stalked round the room in the
warm energies of enthusiasm. Oh what a privilege it is to man to be
enabled to scan the matchless works of Omnipotence. To behold them
and their all-glorious Author is surely the first employment of an
angel. . . .

The gradual filtering down through society of the liking
for country excursions, although it had for some decades
scarcely any share of the limelight, was nevertheless a
continuous process. By 1820 all types, and not merely people
of artistic pretensions, were to be met with among the
belated followers of the fashion: the Corinthian imitator of
Pierce Egan's heroes, airing his urban hooliganism at the
expense (as he hoped) of the unsophisticated country people,
the literary snob, the gaping Londoner, the burgess of
Lancaster or Preston tardily honouring the prophets whose
fame has at last resounded indirectly in their own country,
and the dull fellow, or more often female, who is grateful for
anything that will make him feel busy and in the movement.
Probably most of these types had been visible at the Lakes
from a very much earlier period, but it is by 1820 that their
presence is generally noticeable in literature; that is to say,
after this date the old convention that everyone who visited
the Lakes was something of a bold explorer is finally found
to be worn out, and forgotten.

From now for a long period, admiring scenery remained
a novelty for the middle classes, to be enjoyed rather with
a slight conscious self-approbation. Towards the end of this

SKIDDAW

by William Westall, 1822

HONISTER CRAG

From the lithograph by J. B. Pyne, 1853

stage, appreciation is increasingly recommended in terms of painting. Thus (in 1824) John MacCulloch the geologist, speaking of the Scottish Highlands many of the remoter parts of which he was the first to explore with serious scientific purpose:

> Here too are scenes which do not refuse the painter's art; the compositions being as perfect as they are grand and full of fine detail, and nothing being wanting which can be required for this style of rich landscape. . . . The Tay is seen flowing deep below, amidst the noble oaks which skirt its banks, winding under the prolonged and wild declivities of Craig Vinean, as, bounded by its lofty hills, and displaying the bright meanderings of its river, it terminates in the distant blue summits of the remote Highland.

The yearning for romantic sensation, and the taste for pictures in an already familiar style, had in the first place united to produce the liking for picturesque scenery in nature, which had in turn made popular a style of landscape painting rather more directly derived from nature, and now the process was carried a stage further by people increasingly demanding from scenery the qualities they had learnt to appreciate in 'picturesque' pictures. The earlier romantic element was therefore less, and certain pictorial qualities more, in demand.

To the severe anti-jacobins of MacCulloch's period a mountain could easily be 'more fantastical than pleasing'. Mountains then were not expected to frown savagely, but to go properly attired in purple or blue according to the exigencies of the prospect, forests to wave like the 'wind-swept' coiffure and side-whiskers of a Corinthian buck; or perhaps, a little later, rivers to roll and forests to spread (as one sees in the early lithographs) like the bear's-greased locks of an Early Victorian dandy. But not long after 1825 the movement toward scenery seems to have suddenly lost its intellectual drive, although as a social habit it may have been as widespread as ever. The fact is that the centre of public opinion was changing. As at the beginning of the previous century, people are once again in love with all the works of man. Gas lighting, sanitation, Count Rumford's patent stoves, the partial civilising of the urban mob by the evangelicals and by the new police forces established here and there, and of course, above all, the smell of money, played their part in persuading people that town life was not such a bad thing after all. If the highest degree of improvement and respectability was yet very far from universal, there was the prospect of it in the future even more intoxicating than actuality. Scenery was getting rather Tory in flavour. This change in the centre of gravity was in part due to a relative decline in the social importance of the class to which the cult had most appealed in its earlier days. The artistic idealism which had given it birth and which had been implied in the vast programmes of landscape planning of the past could only have been the fruit of a well-settled comfortable society. Payne Knight is typical in his circumstances. Now the traditions and tastes of the old upper middle class were being overwhelmed by the numbers of new rich on the one hand, and by new movements and causes on the other. The idealism of the new age was forced into more practical channels. It had never been the people who were most nearly affected by the squalor of the early industrial age who had reacted most strongly against urban conditions. Green of Manchester is the nearest instance we have to the contrary, almost the only one. This is to be expected, as it is always the best-nourished, and not the most oppressed, who form the shock-troops of a revolution. Country squires and parsons, and such as Thomas Love Peacock's 'Captain Fitzchrome', or at least the professional classes, had made up most of the early tourists, whilst those who lived in insanitary conditions in the new manufacturing towns, callous to their discomforts and ugliness, had their own amusements. It seemed likely to Wordsworth, writing in 1844, that if the urban masses were let loose in the Lakes, those who catered for them would only reproduce there the bull-baiting, shin-paring, cock-fighting and drunken rowdiness of an old English holiday. He himself, who had once raised his standard with the sea and the mountains as twin emblems of liberty, now ranked as an elderly Tory. After all, whatever was the liberty he had dreamed of, it never was the liberty to bring the manners and customs of the Black Country to Grasmere. But in so far as he thought that change of place does not necessarily change the man, and that mankind is really only amended one at a time, he was right enough.

Punch, that indispensable source of social history, was to begin its life in 1841—as a Radical paper. For its first decade and a half it contains hardly a single mention of the picturesque, and very little of any of the interests of the older world such as sport, scholarship, or taste in gardening. (As well search the *Tribune* for articles on the design of golf courses or collecting first editions.) Its staple topics are the defalcations of railway directors, urban entertainments, political personalities, and the necessity for public health legislation. The physical dangers of railway travel are repeatedly aired, but travel as a topic in itself attracts no attention or interest. Not until about 1885 does *Punch* take notice of the fact that quite ordinary persons spend their Sundays in trying to get away from bricks and mortar. When at last it does, its attitude is perfectly sympathetic to them.

The new class of urban tourists, risen from the ranks of industry and commerce, was catered for by a new *Guide to the Lakes* published in 1855: that of Harriet Martineau, herself a prominent member of what Peacock had called the Steam Intellect Society. Although political economy and social observation keep cheerfully breaking through from time to time, it is a gay and readable little book. In the second quarter of the nineteenth century, in that age of vigorous social ebullition and unstable social foothold, it had been important for the upward swimmer to imitate the motions of the older-established fauna still dominant on the surface of respectability; but as for the inner spirit, that was another matter. The busy and prosperous Lakeland scene had already, in 1840, received the accolade of a Royal visit, if only of the widowed Adelaide. But, though people like the neighbours to know that they have made the tour of the Lakes, whilst they are there what they really want is to enjoy themselves vigorously and to see value for their money. People do not now, in 1855, distress themselves or others much about whether their taste is correct. They swallow the country in big gulps. The elders and the girls in hired 'cars' make 30-mile drives round the fringes of the mountains, ticking off as they pass them the names of the owners of the better villas and mansions, whilst the young men—yes and the girls too, if they like—walk the fifteen or twenty miles across the passes to join them by a short cut. I suspect that very few youth hostellers nowadays normally walk—actually walk—so far in the Lakes.

These business types have a keen eye for character, and pawky stories about the native people are well received. But the old fantasy of the Simple Children of Nature is quite discarded. The Lake District, so many times 'touched with the finger of Taste', by so many authors, is now prodded rudely by the finger of Political Economy. Although it is only fair to say that Harriet is not usually ill-natured, one passage is almost frightening:

> The linen and woollen webs woven by (the peasant) his wife and daughters would not sell, except at a loss, in the presence of the York- shire and Lancashire woollens and cottons made by machinery. He became unable to keep his children at home, leaving home yet more cheerless, with . . . more temptation to drink. Having reached this pass, it is clearly best the process should go on till the primitive population, having lost its safety of isolation and independence, and kept its ignorance and grossness, shall have given place to a new set of inhabitants.

Here we may digress a moment to notice one considerable change which had been made in the mountain landscape about the end of the first quarter of the nineteenth century. Landscape changes, within the limits of our story, are few, and in the aggregate not by any means over- whelming: a little coniferous planting, a very little major draining, and, when family labour was plentiful, there was less bracken than we see nowadays, and more small patches of arable, especially oats. The growth of mansions and gardens is the biggest single change. Now came the division of the uplands, or of a substantial portion of them, into the big 'fell allotments' formed out of the old commons, under the Inclosure Acts. The tall, ruthlessly straight, well-built walls of this era, so different from the ancient, rambling, boulder-built walls near the villages, speak eloquently of the Georgian squirearchy who carried through these schemes, armoured and confident in their triple bronze of political influence, legalism, and ruling ability. It is interesting that the Tory Wordsworth, whose aesthetic principles, both personal and received, ought to have revolted against this carving up of the landscape, holds his peace, and that the aesthetic protest is left to Miss Martineau, whose economic beliefs must have suggested unqualified approval.

'The stranger has now made his three tours. There is one thing more that he must do before he goes on into Cumberland. He must spend a day on the mountains.' But now attend: '*If alone, so much the better.*' Harriet could reason; but she could also feel, and see. Yet the desideratum of exploring the wilderness for oneself has to be qualified by numerous warnings about the dangers of attempting the bigger mountains without a guide. Scafell, Helvellyn (at least from Patterdale) and even Old Man, were all in this category. But why? Not for lack of energy—Miss Martineau was herself a keen walker. Not because of insubstantial romantic qualms, for she mocks at the sensational accounts of mountain climbing 'sixty years since', at the gentleman who was 'so astounded with the different appearance of objects in the valley beneath' that he 'wished to lose blood and return'.

There was really a good deal to be said for her view. Fatalities did happen, do happen. The rambler-trodden paths of to-day, and the many cairns, did not exist, and there was no kind of ambulance or rescue organisation, so that an accident in itself slight might well end in death from exposure. The general conditions indeed more nearly resembled those of to-day in the remoter Scottish Highlands. After all, the Victorians, before climbing their mountain, had probably walked at least half a dozen miles to the foot of it, and without complaint. Their equipment, their foot-gear, their maps, were far inferior to our own. Elementary mountain and travel experience was less disseminated. Consider how an expedition such as Sir John Franklin's one to the Canadian North had miserably perished, about the time Miss Martineau was writing, in country partially inhabited by Eskimos, through ignorance of what every undergraduate explorer now knows. When companions of similar interests were fewer, and local guides readily available, her warnings amounted to little more than the advice, very salutary as applied to the general mass of tourists, not to adventure singly over ground whose character they did not know. It is pretty evident, on her own showing, how frequently this prudent advice was defied. So perhaps ends the great debate about why our ancestors failed to cope with mountains (or the nearest thing that we have to mountains, in this country), and perhaps with the conclusion that in hardihood and vigour they were not inferior at all, but from force of circumstances superior to ourselves.

The very people Miss Martineau wrote for may be seen in the engravings after J. B. Pyne, which were published two years earlier, in 1853. These were produced in styles to suit every pocket and in varying sizes. The finest edition is richly coloured, and, technically at least, a triumph. It is not the intention of this book to indulge in the sport of guying the Victorians, or anyone else; and though the introductory blurbs to the prints are not to be taken too seriously, yet anthropologically they are good evidence. It seems that mankind has now arrived at a concordat with nature; one cannot say a harmony. Gents in top hats and ladies in shawls with parasols sit in holiday mood, yet always dignified, in row-boats whose ample lines assure the triumph of humanity over the mischievous propensities of wind and water. Bottles float innocently in the water, and in the background urchins are more than suspected to be lodged in the forks of the trees. Elsewhere rustics appear, gracefully disposed indeed, but engaged in honest work—for this is no *Derby Day* or *Paddington Station* but a fifteen-guinea record of an important personal pilgrimage. The mountains are encouraged to behave in character, for in several plates there are lightning flashes harmlessly sporting in the distance; but westward look! there is always calm benign weather in the same picture: 'The artist has thrown a golden halo over (Keswick) this city of poets.' Lakes are shown so that their full sweep is displayed, as a salesman displays a dress fabric. One thinks of the old-fashioned restaurants which used to advertise: 'As much as ever you can eat, for half-a-crown.'

'This city of poets'—all of them who mattered had, by now, passed into those realms of gold (on the other side of the epitaph) which publishers, pedagogues and journalists in fealty to poets hold. 'The genius of a Wordsworth, a Southey, a Coleridge, a Wilson, and a Hemans': henceforward they mutely serve, along with de Quincey, Thomas Arnold and the rest as in an open-air department of Madame Tussaud's exhibition; not quite mutely, perhaps, for a few words from them are not amiss whenever it is desired to point a landscape outlook or adorn a carved napkin ring. It is interesting that they have grown in moral stature: 'It is surely agreeable to make oneself acquainted with the local habitation of writers . . . the tenor of whose lives has not belied the honourable characteristics of their works.' This was not the fault of Wordsworth himself, nor of Miss Martineau, who had much too vigorous a mind for such mooning. By right of survivorship, and, like Queen Victoria and George III too, by length of days, 'the virtuous Wordsworth' had before his death in 1850 become a national institution, and, more than this, had very largely lifted with himself on to the safe raft of respectability the whole profession of poet, which, looking back over history generally, one cannot claim to have been normally among the best-reputed, however dear to the gods. Here it remained for quite forty-five years from his death. This was a fine achievement for the group of restless young people of genius, hardly more than averagely well-conducted or happy, who had chanced to settle in the Lakes so long ago; and the thought of it should be very encouraging to anyone who is suffering from the pains of being young.

The popular build-up of Wordsworth as a figure impassive as a Buddha, innocuous as the statuary round the base of the Albert Memorial, must no doubt have corresponded to some emotional need of that age, the more obvious character-istics of which were brisk ebullition up and down the social scale along with a desire to forget the revolutionary and romantic fervours of the previous two generations as well as the outworn restrictions and hoary abuses which had pro-voked them, in its haste to turn to account the opportunities for making money. All the same, these prints of Pyne are a very jolly possession, and the craft of smooth dramatic picturesque draughtsmanship never better understood. But did not The Picturesque formerly imply a concoction whose ingredients were The Beautiful and The Sublime? and did not The Sublime approach nearly to the numinous? In these pictures, there is nothing at all to suggest the last. The Langdale Pikes indeed frown and display their lightnings, but no one need be frightened. The virtuous poets have amply attended to all that. But perhaps Mr. Wordsworth, if he had been still alive, would have felt he had been right about the Windermere railway.

The intercommunication of scenery, social life, and literature at this time cannot be developed here as fully as I should like, but there is room for differences of opinion, and it is better to let people solve this equation as they please rather than be too dogmatic. This time, however, is a caesura, a watershed in our story. The original mine of romanticism is worked out. Society itself is nearing the crest of its secular wave. Behind are the Jacobins, the Regency, the Edinburgh reviewers and the Chartists; ahead is the

THE MIDDLE CLASSES IN OCCUPATION: WINDERMERE

Lithograph by J. B. Pyne, 1853

EARLY VICTORIANS ON THE FELL TOPS

Buttermere from Brandreth, by J. B. Pyne, 1853

constantly accelerating rush of progress and success, down to 1914. Lyell and Darwin have already observed the facts which will shake the authority of Genesis, but in spite of abundant snippets of geological information in Pyne's letter-press, no one has yet pointed out their implications to the top-hatted holiday-makers. The bourgeois rule, and though the poor are always with us, radicalism is quiet. Steam and political economy have triumphed with Martineau; Rawnsley with his preservationism, hand-loom weaving and Keswick *repoussé* work are yet far off. Wordsworth, especially the later Wordsworth, is enthroned; although the spirit of Robert Burns, like some leader of the resistance in the maquis, lurks in the background minds of labouring men, (as can be seen much later, for good or ill, in the work of such as the Denwoods of Cockermouth). The picturesque is dead; long live the new picturesque.

CHAPTER XVII

THE KNIGHT-ERRANT OF DULWICH

To WORDSWORTH, rusticity was a discipline, not a diversion. Much more typical of the nineteenth-century tourist or settler was John Ruskin. The length of his life (1819-1900) spans the gap between the last of the romantic revival and a phase of local society still remembered. It was not until his declining years that he came to live in the Lake District, but the writings and activities of his middle life influenced at many points the growth of the newer romanticism which is now our story. Here again there is no need for us to become too deeply involved in the tangles of criticism. If the Devil can find scripture for any purpose, expression can likewise be found among the 35 volumes of Ruskin's Collected Works for many inconsistent views, and now that they no longer confuse contemporary discussion there is little profit in dissecting them for demonstration. Dogmatic as they seek to be, it is not for their dogmas but for their expression of an intense personality that we now read them.

As a child, he was several times taken to the Lakes in their comfortable post-chaise by his parents, typically Georgian travellers after the pattern set by Gilpin and Gray. It is curious to see how that tradition was, by the agency of their famous son's eloquence, wealth, and length of days, further popularised and handed on to a different class in a different age. He stands as the prototype of the rich (but respectable) and highbrow middle-class sightseer, the patron of good unostentatious inns, the practiser of sanely hygienic though not athletic living; wearing as the badge of his justification his interest in the approved kinds of exotic culture which Ruskin himself so busily and effectually popularised. His influence did much to stereotype the ostensible or recognised

interests of travel, for the less adventurous bourgeoisie
of nineteenth-century England, down to 1914 at least.
He was thus the ancestor of the touring motorists, who in
their generation and their fashion rediscovered the English
countryside in the nineteen-twenties. He was like many of
them too in his restlessness arising from social discontent or
failure to solve one's personal problems. Chronically he
wished himself elsewhere or otherwise employed than he was.
Thus, to practising artists he would recommend geology, or
as Slade professor of Fine Art he would lead his students to
wield pick and shovel. Fleeing from industrial England he
would botanise or would dream of grandiose public works in
Savoy; and in Savoy would collect pebbles and gestate
exhortation for folk in Sheffield. This note of neurosis in his
utterances was perhaps what gave it the power to penetrate
sympathetically and to disturb so deeply, in an age which
in its rush to industrial success had developed lopsidedly and
failed to solve so many of its social and cultural problems.

More than anything he actually wrote or did in reference
to the Lake District, it is the general atmosphere of rich-
textured rentier culture, of slightly screw-loose highminded-
ness, which took root here as congenially as the rhodo-
dendrons, and came to seem as characteristic. It was indeed
to very much the same section of the English upper class as
that which was most disposed to the romantic joys of
mountain scenery and seclusion, that his evangel made its
appeal.

Ruskin's inherent receptivity to the picturesque first found
consciousness on a visit to Derwentwater when he was a
child of $5\frac{1}{2}$: 'The first thing that I remember as an event in
life was being taken by my nurse to the brow of Friar's Crag,
Derwentwater. The intense joy mingled with awe that I had
in looking through the hollows in the mossy roots over the
Crag into the dark lake has associated itself more or less with
all twining roots of trees ever since . . . at the creation of the
world for *me* in Friar's Crag, Derwentwater.'

Ruskin saw the Lake District next when aged 7, then at

11, 18, 19, 29, and at 30 when he spent his honeymoon there. After this he did not again visit the Lakes until middle age, when he had purchased Brantwood. In *Praeterita* he tells us that in the northern tour of 1837—his first university long-vacation one—he felt for the last time that pure childish love of nature which Wordsworth ('so idly', as Rawnsley remarks with, for him, unusual sharpness) takes for an intimation of immortality. Says Ruskin: 'It is a feeling only possible in youth, for all care, regret, or knowledge of evil destroys it, and it requires also the full sensibility . . . the conscious strength of heart and hope.'

Ruskin here places this loss of sensitivity as early as his undergraduate days. This is mere self-pity. During the succeeding ten years, whatever his more inward troubles, he was leading a full life of intellectual and social activity, and at the same time of luxury, and of freedom from all the worries connected with the lack of money. His acute awareness of social inequality belonged to the future: The 'care' and 'knowledge of evil' of which he speaks are therefore a little overdrawn, and we may wonder if they need really interfere so disastrously with pleasure in landscape?—although a sense of guilt might do so. He was, moreover, essentially a poet, not, as he liked to think, an omniversatile philosopher, and his strength lay in receptiveness and expression, not in reflection or introspection. No doubt he gives to his passing and personal feelings about scenery a general significance they will not support. Happily, his delight in nature did not turn out to be irrecoverable and few besides himself would have been surprised to find it so: 'I find that by keeping long away from the hills, I can in great part still restore the old childish feeling about them, and the more I live and work among them, the more it vanishes.' Well, surely, to expect to keep one's impressions permanently at the strength of their first impact is asking too much.

Ruskin's busy life, with its many professional, sensuous and social interests, would sufficiently account for his prolonged

PILLAR ROCK, ENNERDALE

The influence of Whymper's *Scrambles among the Alps*

Published by J. Garnett, Windermere about 1870

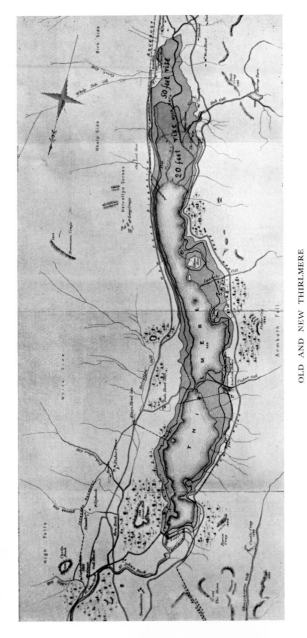

OLD AND NEW THIRLMERE

The effects of raising the former lake 20 and 50 feet are shewn by shading

absence from the Lakes in his middle years. But also we have
to reckon with his desire to come fully to terms with the adult
world and to put these childish associations away from him,
a task which, beginning with his unsatisfactory marriage,
was for him not without great stress and a real attempt
at self-discipline. As he passed his prime he fell back on
the impressions and tastes which had helped to form his
mind.

The Friar's Crag quotation makes clear the way his spirit
worked—he was one of those who live in their visual
impressions. No doubt these impressions in some cases owe
their strength to emotions which have been repressed, but
so distinct, so pleasurable, so fruitful can be these early
memories that it is hard to believe they are nothing but the
shadow of something else. They can also be of a terrifying
kind—the original terror or pain is consciously present only
in the symbol.

This last kind of impression can react long after with un-
suspected strength on the judgment and behaviour of the
man concerned. In Ruskin's case, Wilenski has isolated such
manifestations as an obsessional hatred of small moving
points of fiery light against a dark background, which had
important practical consequences on several occasions in his
career; as for example in the violence of his attack on
Whistler's 'Battersea Bridge', and also in his dislike of
Rembrandt's work. It helps too to explain his special dislike
of railways and of railway travel. His chiding of those visitors
to him who needlessly travelled by rail, and his preference,
to the last, for making even long journeys in his post-chaise,
are part of his Lake District legend. His dislike of railways,
however, was not mainly aesthetic or neurological, but, like
Wordsworth's, political, or social. In his preface to R.
Somervell's *Protest Against the Extension of Railways in the Lake
District* (1877) he wrote:

I am far less interested than my friend in this local and limited
resistance to the elsewhere fatally victorious current of modern folly,
cruelty, and ruin. When the frenzy of avarice is daily drowning our

K

sailors, suffocating our miners, poisoning our children, and blasting the cultivable surface of England into a treeless waste of ashes, what does it really matter whether a flock of sheep, more or less, be driven from the slopes of Helvellyn or the little pool of Thirlmere filled with shale? Little to anyone, and nothing to me. No-one need charge me with selfishness for defence of these mossy hills.

Ruskin disliked industrial civilisation not for the dams, the telegraph poles, the roads which it brought, but for itself, root and branch. Usury, greed, and exploitation were no more tolerable in Manchester than in the Lake District. In the pamphlet quoted he speaks of 'the certainty of the deterioration of the moral character in the inhabitants of every district penetrated by a railway'. It cannot be said that he began the idealisation of the native dalesman character, although he to some extent subscribed to it. In a time when class distinctions, at the beginning of their break-up, were felt with acute uneasiness and a sense of social guilt, many were glad to pick on this sector of humble life—a small, distinct and exotic one, to which rather lush sentiment could be attached without complicating the general issue. To Gray, socially conventional and perfunctory, the dalesmen had merely been, for literary purposes, the simple children of (classical) nature. To Wordsworth's cold eye, inwardly absorbed, the neighbours with whose like he had been acquainted since childhood were the inevitable basis of his moralised and improved examples.

> Shepherds, dwellers in the valleys, men
> Whom I already loved:—not verily
> For their own sakes but for the fields and hills
> Where was their occupation and above.

But to Ruskin, warmer-hearted and much more sociable than either, 'there are men working in my own fields who might well have fought with Henry V at Agincourt, without being discerned from among his knights. . . . What effect, on the character of such a population, will be produced by the influx of that of the suburbs of our manufacturing towns? . . .

I don't want to let them see Helvellyn while they are drunk.'*

In 1871, without having seen it, Ruskin bought Brantwood, on the east side of Coniston Water. He was fortunate in so doing, as its repair and arrangements thus were complete when he had need of it as a retreat in his mental illness, the first signs of which, though unrecognised, were making themselves felt. In such modifications as cornerwise balconies and Italianate windows, naturally the house bears marks of his tastes. Here, his bright blue eyes shining, and both hands outstretched, he welcomed his guests. Here, through happy years of semi-retirement, he pursued his scientific hobbies (which somehow all seemed to evaporate in rhetoric); collected specimens (of course to be ultimately for the Guild, the Rosebuds, the Museum, for anyone but himself); ordered his wine merchant to send cases of the best champagne to his neighbours; accepted in return asparagus, oysters, or some particularly delectable red-currant jelly; or 'undertook to help the clergy of the district, or such as cared to be helped, to what he conceived to be a right understanding of the Lord's prayer'. From here he inspired others to carry out social-economic experiments characterised by deep earnestness, but not always by the same success as the National Trust; and even here in this remote hide-out the Master was occasionally embarrassed by troops of disciples unexpectedly arriving, perhaps with a programme of glee singing in his honour.

After 1878 he made increasing use of Brantwood, and from 1889 onwards, a broken man, he hardly left the place till he died in 1900. The quiet woods, the quiet lake, the majestic mountain opposite, gave him their comfort; whilst, along with vitality, the pain of unassimilable memories and baffled struggles slowly faded. His wife Effie, whose only

* So, later, the author of *Afforestation in the Lake District*, although maintaining that their virtue is due to their alleged Norse heredity, still in this radio age desires to preserve them from themselves by offering them no temptation to depart from 'the traditional sheep farming, the Herdwick breed'.

interest for us nowadays is her high fortune in sharing for a while the name of a genius, was as if she has never been. Some of his foibles, his dogmatism, dilettantism, and even his gastronomy, are fair material for criticism; his attacks from time to time of acute insanity are in a different category. Fortunately he could not foresee the carrion-feeding appetites of biographers four decades after his death. If he was hounded by guilt—the double guilt of great riches and of varying in temperament from the ordinary run of people— few have made fuller expiation: two fortunes given away, a whole generation deeply influenced, and a devoted band of friends witnessing to his personal charm, sense of fun, accessibility, and kindness. Let it not be thought that this chapter has merely been concerned to mock or belittle him— here at Coniston lies one, crazed yet gentle, courteous although unhappy, of fame and influence hardly less wide than that of the Knight of La Mancha.

CHAPTER XVIII

THIRLMERE

IN THE SECOND HALF of the nineteenth century the greatest battle on the picturesque front was over Thirlmere. The journalistic skirmishing took place from the end of 1877, leading up to the hearings before the Select Committee of the Lords in 1878 and of the Commons in 1879. Dr. Goodwin, Bishop of Carlisle, and Dr. Fraser, Bishop of Manchester, were champions on opposite sides, and the national Press was warmly engaged. The proposal to convert the lake into a reservoir for Manchester, 97 miles away, was the first on such a large scale in England or Wales, although Loch Katrine was already supplying water to Glasgow, and in our own district Whitehaven was obtaining a comparatively small quantity of water from Ennerdale Lake. A Thirlmere Defence Association (to oppose the scheme) was formed, which included the names, then not so well known as later, of Octavia Hill and H. D. Rawnsley.

To Ruskin, on the other hand, constructional and civil engineering schemes, provided he approved of their social purpose, could make a strong appeal. He had given his approval to the annexation of Savoy to France in 1860 on observing French engineers promptly settling to work on embanking the Arve. And in 1869 he was full of a scheme of his own for reclaiming, in the interests of agriculture, some sixty miles in length of the Alpine part of the valley of the Rhone, say 700 square miles as he estimated it:

Here is a motive and an employment which will last to the end of my days. . . . It is to arrest the rainfall that I mean to work. I will take a single hillside, and so trench it that I can catch the rainfall for three average years at once . . . it shall all go into the reservoirs. . . . I must have a great work of fortification at the narrowest point of every lateral valley. . . . When I have done this for one hillside, if other people don't do it for other hillsides, and make the lost valleys of the Alps one Paradise of safe plenty, it is their fault, not mine.

He consulted engineers, and made plans for a loan of four million francs for an aqueduct to Venice, as well as trying to interest the Alpine Club. It is, therefore, surprising to find Ruskin's name also as one of the Thirlmere Defence Committee, but as in the case of his fellow-signatory Thomas Carlyle, who was not specially interested in landscape, political and social antipathy to the Lancashire industrial interests which required the water played the larger part. Ruskin was at this time carrying on a controversy with the Bishop of Manchester on the subject of usury, the connection of which with the capitalistic enterprises which Thirlmere was designed to further is plain. A certain amount of metropolitan prejudice against the pullulating northern towns, with their radicalism and their forward-thrusting municipal projects in this dawn of the Collective Age in the 'seventies, is very noticeable in the Press controversies on the subject of Thirlmere. Ruskin was not very active in the anti-Thirlmere campaign, as he was then passing through a time of severe stress, of which one incident was Whistler's libel action against him; and in February 1878 he entered on the first of his periods of insanity.

With the Thirlmere agitation, we begin in some ways to enter a more recognisably modern climate; the arguments used have much of the tone of those familiar to-day. The picture of the Lake District we get, however, is not the same. Thirlmere was then viewed only by dozens as compared with the thousands who pass it now. The Defence Association rather curiously write as if the principal interests to be protected (as appreciators of scenery) were those of the few neighbouring farmers. One hears of 'the contemptuous indifference to rights' (the rights of 'the Cumberland mountaineers') 'as precious, consecrated by association as strong, as deeply seated, as those which attach the great noble to his ancestral domains' (Harcourt's Death Duties of

1894, the War Agricultural Executive Committees, and many compulsory provisions of the National Parks Act, 1949, were indeed hidden in the womb of time). Visitors are mentioned rather *sotto voce*, as appendages of the 'mountaineers'. One suspects that the Defenders could not forget the arguments used by Wordsworth in connection with the Windermere railway, and that he had by no means welcomed the prospect of the country being overrun by tourists. To some extent, therefore, the Lake Country was still regarded as his personal shrine, or that at least of the simple rustic figures of his poems. Awareness of the newer function of the hills as playground for democracy is certainly not absent, but they feel embarrassment in stressing it. The big battalions of the conurbations were in this matter not ranged, as they are to-day, on the side of the scenery-preservers. Employers and employed, with their Bishop at their head, they demanded the water; those who took the other view tended to be those whom privilege or special education set aside from the industrial community. Scenery-viewing was not yet in vogue as a proletarian pastime.

Parts of the Thirlmere basin had been up to this time pretty closely preserved, by the landowners. One diverting scene is that of a party of Manchester aldermen and engineers, who had been warned off by Mr. Leathes of Dalehead Hall, subsequently reconnoitring on hands and knees in the muddy fields, and, round the corner of a wall, meeting a party of their comrades similarly engaged. Truly Manchester has had her revenge.

The scheme at last authorised, provided for raising the water-level fifty feet from the old level of 533 feet above the sea. This increased the area of the lake from 330 to 793 acres, and extended it a little more than a mile to the south. A feature of the old lake was the causeway which crossed it between Dalehead Hall and Armboth, and which included several short detached lengths of bridging, consisting of simple wooden spans between pairs of dry-stone piers. This was delineated on many old prints, on most of which three bridges are shown, but on some two. Between the lengths of bridge, the causeway was much lower, and, no doubt, flood-water used to pass over it. The track thus undulated steeply at each bridge, so that carts forded the shallows alongside the bridges, which in any case were then only wide enough for foot-passengers. In a late photograph, however, no less than six separate bridges are shown. Did the two or three bridges shown in the earlier prints represent an almost unconscious, although unanimous, artistic simplification? The truth seems to be that there originally were only three, or possibly two bridges, but that later the whole causeway was raised and thus it was necessary to make additional openings for the flood-water. The raising of the level also resulted in two rocky knolls becoming islands, one now separated from the shore by 15 feet depth of water and the other by about 30 feet.

On style and points, debating honours were divided between Octavia Hill and John Graves, Chairman of the Manchester Water Committee. The Bishop of Carlisle had complained of 'the substitution of engineering contrivance and utilitarianism for nature in her most primitive and untouched beauty'. To this Graves replied:

> Nature has been at work for ages destroying her most primitive and untouched beauty. Perhaps he prefers the swamps and bogs which Nature always tends to make whenever she has a chance (and never removes again except by great convulsions) to the primitive state when they did exist, or to the artificial conversion of them into dry land.

He went on to explain that the lake had been filled up for a mile and a half at its head by detritus and alluvium.

> The flat ground which has thus been crowded out of the lake—not even planted, as at Ullswater, but divided into fields by straight stone walls—would be a swamp if the streams through it were not artificially embanked. All that ground will be again submerged.

Apart from the particular merits of the Thirlmere land-scape, Graves' letter raises other questions about the enjoy-ment of scenery, which come near to the root of the matter.

Nature is both a cunning craftsman and a heavy-handed
destroyer, and we can take delight in both aspects. The
appearance of complex planning which is evident within the
organism, or the ordered perfection of the crystal, is contrasted with the grisly ruthlessness and disorder of erosion
and predation. The former amounts to beauty, in the old
sense of that word, and stands to many people as proof of a
supernatural Mind. But the other aspect too, sublimity (to
give it its old name), can startle us out of our daily round
of small concerns and set free our imagination. The due
combination of both, in doses and proportions suitable to
our subjective needs, constitutes the picturesque. But compared with reflections along either of these lines, more recent
arguments about whether telegraph poles ought to be of
wood, or of galvanised steel, or whether blue earthenware
ridge tiles should be permitted on buildings, or if ruberoid
shingles, dusted with green slate fragments to imitate natural
slate, are preferable to corrugated sheeting, may seem rather
fiddling matters.

How far Thirlmere was improved or spoiled by the
engineering operations is a question about which people
will have strong predispositions, though it need not be
regarded as beyond reasoned argument. Discussion of
aesthetic principle in landscape matters has not attained
much development, or even maintained its level, since
Payne Knight, Uvedale Price and Repton were engaged in
it more than a hundred years ago, so that we need be the
less afraid of making suggestions of a rather casual sort.
Photographs and descriptions seem to indicate that before
the alterations Thirlmere was not one of the more beautiful
of the lakes, at any rate if one leaves the surrounding hillsides
out of account. Several of the most charming lake-sides are
in fact just those with which the hand of man has had a
great deal to do, removing the bareness and giving them
variety. A large lake is a prime feature in a landscape, and,
unless nature has given it a really adequate setting of the
wild and sublime kind, it cries out to be treated as the

centrepiece of man's design for habitation; that is, in cases where man's occupancy is noticeable in its vicinity at all. The juxtaposition of a lake with mere flat pasture, tame without richness, may be felt to be disappointing. We are always greedy for a little more water in landscapes than nature provides; at least, that is, after the first stage of agricultural taming and draining is complete. Lakes seldom fill their valleys as fully as imagination demands.

In this case the lake was much more than doubled in area. The close approach of its edge to the crags must have greatly improved it as scenery; and its wildness must have been accentuated by the disappearance of the mile, or rather more, of pasture-land at its head. The older ordnance map shows this to have been divided into bare rectangular fields by rather an excessive number of walls, which could scarcely have been beautiful. Scarcely any buildings lie under the water, though several have been allowed to fall into ruin above the present lake edge.

There has been a great deal of rather unreasonable, not to say unscrupulous, criticism of Thirlmere, from the time of the original opponents, who spread the rumour that the water was not fit to drink, down to those who dislike conifers, those who publish trick photographs to demonstrate a theory that the rise and fall of the lake produces unsightly edges (as if even a big lake like Windermere, or a small one like Elterwater, were not each capable of rising and falling six or seven feet) and those who claim that reservoirs are short-lived anyway because they get silted up. Whatever may be true of other regions of the world, or where muddy glacial torrents are concerned, such silting in our climate is likely to take thousands of years, and the untidiness of lake margins where the water-level is variable is hardly to be compared with that of any sea-shore.

In 1892, with the dam at long last complete and the aqueduct to Manchester about to be opened, it is pleasant to find the lion and the lamb lying down together. At the official lunch, the toast of the Manchester Waterworks

Committee was proposed by Rawnsley, who had already opened the aqueduct with an eloquent prayer, and who had written for the occasion no less than four sonnets, one of which he introduced into his speech. With the blessing, in this wise, of the man who was shortly to become the first Secretary of the National Trust, the Manchester Corporation might consider itself absolved, and admitted into the bosom of Cumbrian society.

What exactly had brought about this change of heart is not altogether clear. The invasion of the navvy army was by no means found to be as devastating to peace and morals as had been feared, and the obvious propriety of a good water supply for a million people was an argument the weight of which told more and more with time for reflection. Although a vehement spirit, Rawnsley was a man of the world, a man of goodwill; his instinct was to bridge differences, not to found an intransigent esoteric cult. No doubt he was ready to meet half-way the desire of the Manchester people to behave as tactfully as possible.

The planting around Thirlmere has been done with a good deal of care, but I for one do not feel larch trees to be at all offensive either singly or in armies—or in need of concealment. The subtle dull rose or ochre hues of the different varieties, the massed intricacy of their branches, are to me, descending Dunmail Raise at the end of winter, a note of joyous excitement, whilst their emerald in early spring, at first the suggestion of a green mist, then at last a colour of unexcelled purity and gaiety, makes the heart leap, as the rainbow, or the daffodils, did Wordsworth's. The darker conifers deepen the colour-scale of the landscape, making water seem more richly green or blue by their reflection or shadowing, helping in autumn to balance the red of the bracken.*

* The Dower Report of 1945 did as a matter of fact suggest afforestation as an economic remedy, compatible with scenic amenity, for the bracken infestation of the rough and steep lower slopes and intakes, so difficult to deal with by other means.

Surely the glimpse of water through trees is one of the most entrancing in nature. All over the world do we find forests acting as bastions to mountains. If the close-set forests make less obvious and more arduous the way up the lower slopes, this is only giving back to our over-domesticated and sheep-tamed hills some of their birthright of difficulty and mystery, and augmenting their scale by helping to set apart the genuinely wild upper regions from the humanised valleys.

CHAPTER XIX

NEO-WORDSWORTHIANS

IN THE EIGHTEEN-EIGHTIES, a decade which by way of evocative description has been variously labelled 'earnest', 'soulful', or 'aesthetic', the early stirrings of the countryside preservation movement obtained their drive from the sense of social responsibility felt by the mellowing upper middle class: the pupils, perhaps, of Arnold (Thomas),* and the readers of Arnold (Matthew). Was it then that the Age of Victoria yielded its ripest vintage?—the crudely vigorous stocks thrown up by the Industrial Revolution now beginning to take on the colours of civilisation, whilst the fruit of the maturer social trees was as yet unfallen on the boughs, although swayed by the breath of new winds. As we may see from their portraits in *Punch*, the distinctions of citizen and landowner, gentleman and tradesman, townsman and countryman, ancient in English history and admitted on both sides, were still real, though becoming much confused with one another. There too we may see the contemporary urban background as one of dirt, disease and degradation in a degree we find it nowadays distasteful to contemplate. Civic pride and civic design were, in the mid-century, at an ebb. The amenities of town life were within doors or behind the high walls of private properties; outside was the crossing-sweeper. No doubt things were not really as bad as they appear in those pages. It is the beginnings of change which are spotlighted by the satirist.

The 'preservation' of the Lake District was the responsibility of the dwellers in those large but studiously unpretentious mansions which we have described, built from

---

* Or of his early successors. I have supposed a little time-lag for the establishment of the new spirit in this field. Thomas Arnold died in 1842. Matthew lived until 1888.

the 'fifties or 'sixties onward, Italianate or chalet-style, with their wide eaves, high rooms, and solid, pitchpine verandahs: those houses in which until yesterday the descendants of the great captains and prophets of the Victorian Age lingered, continued to vegetate, up to a ripe old age. The superb outlook to be had from many of these large houses is well worth investigation by the tourist, and will often be quite unexpected though they may be only a short distance from the road. The really extraordinary multiplicity of views is one of the chief charms of our district, and these houses had an early pick. After them, with the approach of the twentieth century, occurs a different and smaller class of house, often built in absolute singlemindedness for the sake of one view. This is a mistake, as the element of surprise is lacking, and such a feature marks them as the work of the offcomer, unassimilated to the country. The quest for the view was sometimes carried to extreme lengths. The huge plate-glass window had the big room built around it; and the rest of the house, as empirical convenience required it, but often regardless of site levels, huddled somehow round the big room. Then, as an afterthought, quaintness would raise its ugly head, a maniac gleam in its eye, and various very unfunctional devices such as minstrel galleries or low exposed beams would waylay the attention of the stranger, somewhat insincerely affecting to link the whole together with a suggestion of native tradition in building. In all of them, in Gothic uncial or in *art nouveau*, in stone, tile, or wood, syncopated or explicit, might be read the legend: *Levabo oculos in montes, unde auxilium meum*.

Typical of the 'earnestness' of the 'eighties were a number of movements in England at large, in which people of upper middle class origin sought to transcend class boundaries without in any way denying their reality. A good example was the housing management scheme of Octavia Hill, whose name we have met in connection with Thirlmere. This scheme was itself suggested and originally financed by Ruskin. Ruskin did not himself by any means have the qualities of the administrator, which are needed to nurse institutions to maturity, but he was able to inspire those who did; and it is fitting therefore that the National Trust should have been founded, in 1895, by two people closely connected with him, Miss Hill and Canon Rawnsley, together with Sir Robert Hunter.

It is interesting to speculate on the precise qualification which earns one a place in the Pantheon of British Worthies, represented by the *Dictionary of National Biography*. Hunter and Miss Hill appear there, but others, either more famous in their own day, like Arthur Orton the Tichborne Claimant, or else of great ultimate influence like Gerard Manley Hopkins, are passed over. Surely few more representative figures could have been found than Hardwick Drummond Rawnsley, whom we seek there in vain.

The character of a great part of Rawnsley's abundant writings appears from the statement of his recreations, given in *Who's Who*: 'Chiefly literary and travel, observations of scenery, bird-life, and habits of animals, and local history and traditions.' As well as some more active pursuits, one might add: 'cherishing the memory of friends'. But that work of reference gives little clue to his many and vigorous activities for the preservation of the scenery of the Lake District.

The influences which originally turned his mind in this direction were apparently those of Thring, the headmaster of Uppingham, and, at Oxford, of Ruskin, under whom he worked on the famous Hinksey Road. Rawnsley's nature was always notable for his generous readiness to undertake the most multifarious practical activities. At the University the influence of Jowett (who nevertheless liked him) was astringent: 'I would not advise you to spend time on verses,' he wrote to England's most prolific future poet. 'You must get rid of all excitable ways which will altogether unfit you for any place of responsibility. No one will tell you the reason, but you will find somehow that you will not succeed in life.'

Rawnsley did not take his advice, but in following his

own bent he carved out for himself a unique niche, almost
that of a Minister of Public Enjoyment and Appreciation.
After a spell of 'muscular Christianity' (as the phrase then
went) at Bristol, he was presented in 1878 to the living of
Low Wray, on Windermere, and in 1883 removed to
Crosthwaite, near Keswick, where he remained nearly up
to his death in 1920. He strove mightily for temperance (as
distinguished from abstinence) in the use of alcohol, and also
to raise the tone of comic postcards, to re-establish maypole
dancing, and to bring art into industry (in the foundation
of the Keswick School of Industrial Art) and to associate
civic life with cathedral worship. At the Diamond Jubilee
he was one of three Joint Secretaries for the nation-wide
plan of bonfires, which numbered 2548. *Punch* in due course
congratulated him on his 30,000th sonnet. The pious
memorial inscriptions he promoted were almost as numerous.
His first act on moving into Crosthwaite rectory was to
have inscribed on a wall some appreciative remarks by
Thomas Gray. On Helvellyn he commemorated the unlucky
Gough, at Grisedale Hause the parting of the Wordsworth
brothers, William Wordsworth again at Cockermouth,
Ruskin at Friar's Crag (with replicas at Coniston Churchyard and Corpus Christi College), the Venerable Bede at
Jarrow, and the ancient poet Caedmon at Whitby. Voices
were heard to question if Caedmon had ever really existed,
but the weight of opinion supported Rawnsley. As a parish
priest he was popular, 'democratic' and 'unconventional'
according to the notions of those days. Once he led a party
of 2000 Keswick people up the hill of Latrigg, armed with
crowbars and other tools, to demolish an obstruction to a
footpath. The curious visitor may still find, on his way up
Skiddaw, the fragments of a drinking fountain of vaguely
ecclesiastical design commemorating this. From the Thirlmere project onwards, he fought in the 'cause' of one piece
of scenery after another, one public right after another—to
protest against a dam on the Duddon, a quarry on Loughrigg, a road round Rydal, an electric tramway to Ambleside,

VICTORIAN THIRLMERE, FROM RAVEN CRAG
Published by J. Garnett

LATE VICTORIAN PORTRAIT:
THE REV. H. D. RAWNSLEY
1851-1920

PEACE

OR THE RAWNSLEYAN PICTURESQUE

by T. Huson, 1894

a sewage works at Windermere, the reconstruction of a
bridge at Portinscale.

Railways too claimed much of Rawnsley's attention. One
line had, as early as 1865, penetrated right through the
northern fringe of the Lake District—the industrially important line from Penrith to Cockermouth which linked the
coke of Durham with the iron ore of West Cumberland. But
this had been in the days of the philistines. In the early
'eighties, a Buttermere Railway Bill was thrown out. The
pertinacious James Bryce, in Parliament, was educating the
public to regard the preservation of wild scenery not merely
as a concern of 'sentimentalist poets and aesthetes' (pejora-
tive words in that age) but as a demand which must be
regularly taken into consideration. As Member first for
Tower Hamlets and then for Aberdeen he made his claim,
not in the name of Wordsworth nor in the name of the
allegedly Wordsworthian peasantry, but frankly on behalf of
the urban masses. The Lake Country now comes to be
described as the 'great picnic-ing ground' which 'the people
(of the manufacturing districts of Lancashire) look on as
their national park'. If this had been all, it would presumably
have been rather hard for Bryce to argue against railways,
then of course the only practicable means of access for the
multitude. His own real feeling, however, was very strongly
for wild and 'unspoilt' scenery. 'Unspoilt'—for at this stage
of the subjugation of nature by mankind, everybody must
have at least begun to wonder where it was all going to end.
Even in the wider spaces of the U.S.A., the Yosemite and
Yellowstone Parks had already been set aside. So Bryce, in
opposition to the members for constituencies concerned, on
more than one occasion carried his point in a pretty full
House, although only by small majorities. The Ennerdale
Railway Bill, in 1884, was the first on which he obtained an
instruction, on second reading, to the Select Committee 'to
enquire whether the proposed railway will interfere with
the enjoyment by the public who annually visit the Lake
District by injuriously affecting the scenery in the neighbour-

L

hood'. But for this, the chairman of the Committee would
have been obliged to rule aesthetic evidence out of order.
The instruction was repeated in the case of the Ambleside
Bill in 1887. But both these bills were thrown out on their
financial and other demerits, without need to invoke the
Instruction, so that we are denied the spectacle of the
magnificent tournament of Aesthete versus Capitalist which
would have ensued, in the Select Committee's proceedings,
and which might have taken rank among the *causes célèbres*
of the century.

It is possible indeed to regret that the railway from
Windermere to Ambleside was not constructed, either by the
local syndicate of promoters of the bill, or by the L. & N.W.
Railway, which several times considered it. If people are to
reach the Lakes by rail, there must be a terminus somewhere,
and the choice of the present Windermere station seems an
odd one. Looking back, it is hard to understand the doubt
which was felt in 1887 about potentialities of traffic. The
route (including its Ambleside terminus) was to have been
well back from the Lake, and a couple of hundred feet above
it, quite out of sight of the main road. The most important
engineering work required was the crossing of the Troutbeck, at a height of 136 feet, just below the house called
Brow.

Rawnsley was the mover in fund after fund, *ad hoc* society
after society, for the preservation of the picturesque. Their
names need not now trouble us, but they pioneered the way
to the organisational technique of later times. One of his
most vigorous agitations was against the proposed mineral
railway from Braithwaite to Buttermere: ·

Are the proprietors who work a certain slate quarry up in Honister
to be allowed to damage irretrievably the health, rest, and pleasure
ground of the whole of their fellow-countrymen who come here for
needed quiet and rest? Let the slate train once roar along the western
side of Derwentwater, and Keswick as the resort of weary men in search
of rest will cease to be.

Nowadays the weary men in search of recreation would

perhaps be working on the restoration of the slate railway as an antique in its own right, like the Portmadoc and Blaenau Festiniog Railway.

Amid all this cheerful bustle of useful activity, literary and polemical, Rawnsley's habitual invocation of peace seems almost a discordant note. In his hands, Wordsworth's 'National Property' becomes 'National Resting-Ground'. He muses over the graves of the prophets, Wordsworth and Ruskin, agreeably sketching in the botanical amenities of the spot to reinforce the congenial mood of gentle melancholy. His contemporary, the poet William Watson, also equates Wordsworth's teaching with peace. To our ears, after two world wars, the intensification of industry and much more strident presentation of news and propaganda, the cry comes strangely. One wonders whatever was the matter with the world at the end of Victoria's reign, that they should feel they needed so much peace. Old photographs of Keswick market-place certainly look peaceful enough. (It is true we do not hear the shouts of the competing wagonette touts; we do not think of the active building development going on just out of the picture, which had already made that town, like others, very different from the one Wordsworth knew.)

It is the thesis of this book that appreciation of rural scenery depends in any period on the tint of the spectacles people bring with them from the towns. The countryman's view of nature, just because it is deeper, is more difficult to separate from his life as a whole—he is, so to speak, a true Wordsworthian in spite of himself. But a man whose life is in and by the country will not feel toward it as the same man would if he merely visited the country by way of recreation; and probably the latter will have much more to say, as one usually does about a subject which makes a fresh impact. It is thus to contemporary urban conditions and national life as a whole that we must constantly look for the explanation of movements of taste in scenery.

In the last two decades of the nineteenth century much misgiving was felt about general principles. The enormous and deserved success of the Early Victorian material development itself suggested a stocktaking. In the wider realms of ideas, apart from the ever-mischievous buzz in the hard-boiled circles of financiers, diplomatists, and politicians, those decades called in question such things as the just basis of society, the position of women, the place of religion in education, and the implied criticism of religion by the advance of biological and archaeological, as formerly by geological, science. Here and there in country parsonages clergymen like Mrs. Humphrey Ward's Robert Elsmere (in Longsleddale) were Tormented by Doubt. Not so Rawnsley, of whom a critic said he 'scarcely knew what he believed about dogmatics; at least he desired beneficence and good feeling to rule the world'. In the midst of the congratulatory eloquence at the opening ceremony of the Thirlmere project, as at Belshazzar's feast, an unaccountable shadow fell, and something strangely prompted the chairman to remark on 'the great questions of the unemployed, of the hours of labour, and of wages, looming in the distance'. But as for Lancashire, it was still going ahead like a steam engine, all progress and brashness: 'What Lancashire thinks to-day, London thinks to-morrow.'

Rawnsley's cry for peace was in the main a social protest against his contemporary world and its march of events. In this he resembled the later Ruskin, but, if with less of Ruskin's intense artist's sensibility, yet more free from the elements of neurosis and self-indulgence. Rawnsley liked mountains but he happened to like ordinary people too. It is his essential service, and due to him more than to any-one else, that the accusations of selfishness in the exercise of privilege, which had visibly and not undeservedly embarrassed the preservers of the Lake District ever since Wordsworth's time, now to some extent lost their sting.

In the big cities there were many factors which made life there more oppressive and confining than to-day, and the contrast between town and country greater. Most conspicuous from our point of view was the non-existence of motor cars to escape from them at will. When Rawnsley came to Wray, the old monstrous London of the stories of Conan Doyle, R. L. Stevenson and Machen, not to say Dickens, was beginning to disappear—romantic novelists always have a tendency to hark back to what is gone—that drab, foggy, mysterious jungle so lacking in public social services and the various systems of spoon feeding and form-filling by which its deepest recesses are now invaded.

The townsmen had their own traditional modes of enjoyment. We recall how Wordsworth doubted whether in the mass they could ever be educated to behave in a seemly manner in the country. Rawnsley's peace, in fact, was very much a new kind of thing in holidays so far as the masses were concerned. After all, walking and admiring scenery and meditating over the graves of the poets are not everybody's cup of tea even now. Would it be right to think of this style of appreciating the Lakes as a belated, minor, and rather esoteric phase of the romantick taste which began with Gray?

One would like to be able to say that the vast social improvement since the mid-nineteenth century has been in a substantial degree due to Wordsworthian philosophy, but one cannot honestly do so. Wordsworthianism is a jealous cult, and does not yield its blessing to those who are merely on the lookout for gratification without being willing to lead the life he indicated. 'Strangers', sneers William, 'not linked to the neighbourhood, but flitting to and fro between their fancy villas and the homes where their wealth was accumulated.' It is perhaps because the real Wordsworthian is the man who has turned his back on the town altogether and has become in some measure deaf to civic ambition and conscience, that attempts to improve town life by injecting a measure of Wordsworthianism into it are apt to be rather sterile. The individual here and there may be inspired, but such ideas are not readily transplantable. The problems of the urban industrial life of the millions have to be solved on its own lines. The improvement since Victorian times has not been due to excursions to the Lakes, but to such things as municipal enterprises, trade union organisation, secondary and technical education, and a long list of things we are not concerned with here. Appreciation of nature may be possibly considered as a pointer on the dial, but not a major influence in the reciprocal direction.

The reasons why, as compared with ourselves, some of the later Victorians so yearned for peace seem therefore to be imperfectly accounted for. The trauma of the Industrial Revolution was perhaps much more severe than we now remember. But, though busy towns had never been quiet, steam and mechanisation did introduce an element of sheer noise which resembled nothing known before. Nowadays of course we are so conditioned to noise everywhere that we find it hard to imagine how at first 'the shriek of the locomotive and the clatter of the train' distressed people. The trials which we their descendants have undergone, so far from beating us into nervous debility, have had the opposite effect of toning up our minds. To take as a parallel the Cumbrian sport of rock-climbing, it is a commonplace that (as in many other sports too), the comparative novices of to-day take quite easily to feats which a generation ago were considered the *ne plus ultra* of severity. It is almost as if the physical endowment of the race had increased, though clearly this cannot really have occurred in so little time. Has something of the same sort happened to us all, in our tolerance of urban life and stress? I think it has, though I cannot explain it in detail. Mankind did *not* find it easy to acclimatise itself to the acceleration of the tempo of industrial and urban life in the nineteenth century, though there is no reason to think that that measure of accomplishment represents anything approaching the limits of its powers of adjustment. What came later was fortunately unguessed. But always

> Lads knew trouble in Knighton
> When I was a Knighton lad.

The purposes to which we now seek to put the Lake District, as rendered available under the National Parks Act, are far more dynamic than the old ideal of a holiday in the Lakes. The shift of emphasis from the contemplative lakes to the ardours of the mountains has been almost total.

CHAPTER XX

THE CLIMBERS

THE CLIMBERS have a very distinctive place in the appreciative exploration of the Lake District. Climbing is a sport, but much more than a sport; it casts a shadow bigger than its own apparent size. In the first volume (1908) of the *Journal* of a climbing club afterwards famous, high claims are made:

> Our sport differs from all others because of the close connection it has always maintained with letters. The books of other sports contain the figures of record performances and the details of competitive results, but the names that are remembered in mountaineering annals are not necessarily those of the strongest and most skilful, but those who have been best able to express the supreme delight to be found among the mountains for them—for some others to be found in music and art.

and further:

> The tradition of mountaineering—and of English climbing—are as inspiring to us as the chapters of history are to a patriot.

Bold words, for a provincial club of only a few dozen members, formed in the preceding twelve months! But to many they would seem no more than indisputable truth.

Who really was it who started rock-climbing in Britain? Undoubtedly it was in the Lake District that it began. As early as 1884 a long article by C. N. Williamson appeared in *Good Words* (that rich treasury, of which odd volumes, with luck, may now sometimes be rescued from street barrows) on 'Climbs in the English Lake District'. By 'climbing' nowadays we mean choosing deliberately a route because it is not easy. Hardly any of these were climbs in this sense, but rather were the easiest routes in inevitably difficult situations, such as Broad Stand on Scafell, or Pillar Rock by the Slab-and-Notch Route. Of course, natural aptitude for scrambling had always existed in individuals, and had been irrepressible, so that many of the earliest recorded exploits in the Lake District were those of solitaries. It is not of them we now speak, but of all that is meant by a tradition, with its pride and exclusiveness, its missionary spirit, its ethics, and its heroes.

Miss Adam Smith has suggested that the sport, in so far at least as it developed from strenuous emulative walking and hill-climbing, owes much to the physical strenuousness encouraged in the youth of the English middle class by Arnold of Rugby. I do not think so, even though at the foot of the Wythburn track up Helvellyn is to be found a memorial stone with verses mentioning one famous walk by members of Arnold's own family. Such men as John Wilson, Joseph Wilkinson or William Green needed no urging from this source, and the exploration of the rougher parts of the mountain country had gone on ever since. Certainly, it was the custom from the middle of the nineteenth century to hold university vacation reading parties in the remoter districts, even in the Scottish Highlands, and the Arnolds may have had some influence here. But for several decades people scrambled as individuals, without a collective tradition, recognised routes, venues, technique or standards of difficulty being established.

Difficult climbing indeed was developed *as a sport* by Englishmen in the Alps, from the 'sixties onward, nearly twenty years before the same thing came about in Britain, and the one thing led to the other. In an article in the *Climbers' Club Journal*, 1955, Mr. E. C. Pyatt has described the beginnings in the Lake District, and has traced the interaction of the various factors. When the two breeds met at Wasdale in the early 'eighties, the native scramblers, it appears, tourists or local, tended to resent somewhat the element of virtuosity introduced by the Alpine men. The deliberate search for difficulty as such, the use of appliances, like ropes, ice-axes and crampons, and the exotic Alpine terminology, stood in contrast to the equally able but less self-conscious reliance on hob-nailed boots and fell-poles, which went with a more catholic and frequently deeper-rooted love of the hills. The new-fangled technique was condemned as likely to be the means of leading climbers of third-rate ability into places where only first-rate natural climbers ought to be, men who could get there and back without advice or help from anyone.

As it happened, it was the native, not the Alpine, school which threw up the first rock-climbing genius, and he it was who obtained a notable plum: the discovery as well as the first ascent of the sensational rock pinnacle which has ever since been adopted as the symbol of rock-climbing in the Lake District. This was the Napes Needle, at Wasdale, which Walter Haskett-Smith climbed in 1886. (Fifty years later, in 1936, he was to climb it again, this time second on the rope, to the acclamation of many friends.) After this achievement, the rival Wasdale coteries rapidly fraternised, and from this time dates the growth of the traditions of the sport. In the twenty years between C. N. Williamson's topical article, and the foundation of the first local club, many standard Lakeland climbing routes were worked out, by such men as O. G. Jones and the Abraham brothers of Keswick. In the first *Journal* the club published, therefore, the sport is already richly patinated, and full of overtones, and we already begin to hear the complaint that the Lake District holds no fresh possibilities for climbing.

But it is not the history of clubs or climbs that interests us here; rather the history of climbers' ideas. Without troubling about statistical fact, let us try to capture a gramme or two of the pure essence, volatile yet how pervasive and powerful. The prominence of the literary bent among climbers is partly explained by the schoolmasters, barristers, and others with long vacations who congregated at such places as Wasdale. In contrast perhaps, were gatherings at Coniston, drawn from young engineers from the shipyards of Barrow-in-Furness, and the exploits of the Abraham brothers of Keswick, which helped to give climbing in the

Lakes that native or grass-roots character it never had in North Wales.

If foxhunting has been called the image of war, then climbing was the image of anarchist revolutionary conspiracy, for which men withdrew from the hated town to secret valleys, foregathered in crowded ill-lit back inn-parlours filled with tobacco smoke, and scornfully hiding their plans from a scornful public, acknowledged as password the exciting new technical jargon of pitches, chimneys, arêtes and chockstones. Desperate as dynamitards, they planned their deeds, calling for utter resolution and loyalty, and, following their leaders, yet in the fullest individual stature, they went forth to do, and to do, and do. There in the upper world, where emptiest air meets earth at its most ironbound, most structural, they danced their solemn dance. To many of them it seemed that the grim partner whose rugosities engaged their finger-tips and a boot-nail or two, and whose attitudes demanded their most intense attentiveness, was actually alive; could wish them ill and destroy them by voluntary act; could also, in accordance with the pathetic fallacy, somehow reflect their joy in the sunshine and in physical effort; could tell them, if she would, the secret of another kind of wisdom more ancient than the human race, more true than flickering human thought. To her, therefore, was their love.

Perhaps we need not go so far as this, but merely note, with Samuel Johnson, that it concentrates a man's mind wonderfully well when he is going to be hanged—or fall a hundred feet, it makes no matter. Hence, one can at least understand 'the emotional resources of escape from the frigid pattern of urban life', and what a potential of force might be engineered to drive, for example, a movement for influencing the development of the mountain country. Little did these young people think, however, that they would one day claim and actually exercise public functions as nominees of the Minister on the Park Planning Authority.

CHAPTER XXI

REGION SEPARATE, SACRED

TO THE RAMBLER OR CLIMBER, it appears self-evident that the beautiful valleys in which he takes his holidays form an entity, apart and independent, not merely from the point of view of tourist facilities but in other ways too. A convenient definition of the Lake District is Wordsworth's, often-quoted from his *Guide*. He requested his reader

to place himself, with me, in imagination, upon . . . the top of either of the mountains, Great Gable, or Scafell, or rather, let us suppose our station to be a cloud hanging midway between those two mountains . . . we shall then see, stretched at our feet a number of valleys, not fewer than eight, diverging . . . like spokes from the nave of a wheel.

He enumerates Langdale, continued by Windermere nearly to the sea; Coniston, the 'broken spoke sticking in the rim' of the imaginary wheel but not touching its centre; then Duddon, Esk, Wasdale, Ennerdale, the Buttermere valley down to Cockermouth, and Borrowdale. But this, he says, is little more than half a circle; so he shifts his centre four or five miles east, to bring into view Wythburn and St. John's Vale, Ullswater, and the vale of Grasmere down to the head of Windermere; and though it cannot be brought into his imaginary panorama, Haweswater is added for good measure.

In regard to the valleys radiating from the mountain centre, this description is, in the first place, a glaciological one. In the next place, it suggests that Wordsworth, in beginning where he does begin, had in mind the volcanic rocks of which the upper parts of the valleys consist: the Borrowdale Series. It is these rocks, a compact block on the map, which offer all the most rugged scenery of the district. But most of the valleys he mentions run down for part of their length, in some cases much the greater part, into areas of older, sedimentary rock: the Skiddaw slates on the north, or the Silurian on the south. Neither of these two geological areas extends widely over England, and both therefore may be considered as, like the Borrowdale Series, characteristic of the Lake District; and no doubt the scenery they produced seemed so to Wordsworth, as it has done to many since. But, because it is less central, and also less wild, this scenery has seemed characteristic in a rather subordinate way. In extending his region to Haweswater on the east, Wordsworth is still within the bounds of the Borrowdale rocks, and still within those of glacial hill-sculpture, though the glaciers which effected it were not those of the main centre in the Scafell-Gable group.

In and about Eskdale there is quite a large area of granite, but it cannot be said that this gives rise very conspicuously to the granite type of scenery—dome-like or slabby—which is usually so easy to recognise elsewhere. The Forestry Commission in the course of a controversy in the 'thirties made a daring attempt to cut out Eskdale from the flock of Lake District dales, on the ground that it had no lake; but the Rev. Mr. Symonds, like a vigilant shepherd, rushed to its defence and the wolf was repelled. His argument, however, that Eskdale was no more deficient in lakes than Langdale, overlooked Blea Tarn, Stickle Tarn, Loughrigg Tarn, Little Langdale Tarn and the tripartite Elterwater, as well as such other lakes as may have existed there since glacial times. (It would have been better to have relied on the canonical text of Wordsworth.) But the aggression has not been repeated.

To this region, the 'separate and sacred', as Sir William Watson called it, the name Cumbria is often applied. The advantage of this name, which has no precise significance, is that it can be made to mean just as much as the speaker wishes. The word indeed is very ancient. It was reported to King Edward I that Cumbria consisted then, and indeed for many centuries before his time, of the bishoprics of Glasgow, Whithorn in Galloway and Carlisle, including the west coast down to the Duddon, and the northern part of

Westmorland, which later became the Barony of Appleby. But nowadays, in common use, the name is equivalent to Wordsworth's Lake District, that is, parts of north and south Westmorland, of Cumberland, and of Furness in Lancashire. Much of the indefinite significance of Cumbria, its incantatory quality, is inherited even by the name of Cumberland.

Thus, in the obituary of Beatrix Potter, the writer of children's books, *The Times* spoke of her home as in Cumberland, although in fact it was in Lancashire, a dozen miles from the modern county of Cumberland. This is not an isolated slip, nor an accidental one, but an unconscious assertion of what it is thought the place-name *ought* to include; and many examples could be found. 'Lancashire' must on no account be mentioned in this sort of connection; its name has no more to do with this field of ideas than the part of the United Kingdom called Northern Ireland has to do with Mr. de Valera's mystical realm of Eire, which likewise overflows the borders of mere actuality, in that case the territory of the Republic of Ireland.

This sort of thing is entirely harmless if it amounts to no more than a preference about what places ought to be called; but the motive is a preference about what places ought to be, a wish to see them otherwise than as they are, and to make them conform to the dream. Given time for the sharing of it, for confidence in its reality to grow, and for an imposing structure of concrete proposals and arguments to be constructed about it, the dream may become a very solid force, an opinion all the more obstinate because of the underlying awareness of its chimerical origin.

In 1936 there appeared a remarkable book, *Afforestation in the English Lake District*, by the Rev. H. H. Symonds. For an appeal of such vehemence, on an aesthetic subject and aimed at a popular audience, one would probably have to go back to Ruskin. Its argument was that coniferous forests, by their dark and uniform colour, and, where planted commercially, their uniform height, make the landscape monotonous. They have little undergrowth or bird-life, and, in establishing them, public rights of way are apt to suffer. The straight lines of their boundary fences and of their fire-breaks are offensive to the eye and tend, so it is said, to dwarf the somewhat miniscule landscape of the district. Much is made in the book of the interference with sheep farming by cutting up the grazings and by the planting of valley land essential for winter feeding, but one feels the real pressure is an aesthetic one. As John Dower pointed out in his report, there is in the district much ground, especially rocky hill-sides, which has become useless to sheep and which can hardly be reclaimed from bracken except by planting, and much even of the sheep ground is of very small economic value.

The book is written sometimes with busy litigiousness, sometimes with passionate rhetoric, and in one or two places with eloquence. It was written very much for an immediate occasion: to oppose certain plans of the Forestry Com-missioners for dealing with land they had acquired in Duddondale and Eskdale, and its shortcomings therefore as a scientific or historical work are not so material. Its strongly partisan temper and its persistent attribution of bad faith and bad motives to public authorities (since carried on through the long series of Friends of the Lake District pub-lications) renders some of it unreadable, and must even have inflicted some damage on the working of democratic government.

But the function of propaganda, like saturation bombing, is to soften up enemy positions and morale, and one cannot expect it to be measured with the care of a verdict. It is perhaps easier to excuse the first charge made in hot blood than the long continuance of such methods year by year after the Friends had become a recognised party to negotia-tions on all questions affecting picturesque amenity. With such objectives, the book has been immensely effective. Propaganda is a weapon of extremely powerful long-term effects irrespective of its crudity apparent at the time of application. Long before the National Parks Act of 1949, any government department whose duties required it to

consider plans for the Lake District must have searched its
conscience urgently before proceeding with them; and it
became the custom with several to seek privately the oracle
from the priest of the wrathful God of the picturesque,
before venturing on any public declaration of policy, from
which it might be difficult to retreat with credit. Whose-
soever may be the fault, several Lakeland valleys remain,
down to the present day, without public electric supply, and
no doubt much marginal and derelict land fails to be
economically utilised in the national interest.

From the point of view of effectiveness, one cannot, however, withhold admiration for the talent for organised agitation which is displayed in this and the succeeding pamphlets.
Afforestation itself opens with a parade of the most prominent
names in various departments of society who had signed a
petition against the Forestry Commission's intentions. 2500
humbler signatures were claimed from the parts of Westmorland, Cumberland and Lancashire reckoned to belong to the
Lake District, together with the more populous remaining
portion of the county of Cumberland, and another 13,000
signed from the rest of England. More important, however,
in the long run, than signatures on a particular occasion,
was the technique of infiltrating and affiliating various clubs
and societies, big and little, formed for rambling, climbing
and so on, so that the aspect of a solid and permanent body
of opinion was thus created. Such an affiliation might in the
first place mean little more than a rather general expression
of goodwill toward the preservation of picturesque amenity,
coupled with a wish to maintain liaison, but subsequently
the affiliated are apt to get a sort of vested personal interest
in the policy followed, until by force of habit it becomes an
article of faith.

In these ways were linked varieties of sentiment and
fantasy on the one hand to a powerful talent for organisation
and political pressure on the other. Sentiment was focussed
by a distinct boundary prominently drawn round a proposed
National Park, as big as a county, a feature which began to

appear in the Friends of the Lake District publications about 1935. This new county was to be based, not like all preceding areas of dominion, on centres of habitation, but on mountain tops. Mr. Symonds provided for this mystical realm a chosen people, 'the proud and independent dalesmen' whose Norse blood he claimed to own little admixture of Celtic or English; who live by a separate and sacred hereditary craft, shepherding the Herdwick breed of sheep (which their Norse ancestors are said to have introduced and, as it were, patented) and who are stated never to have been conquered by the Normans. A few humans are indispensable in so big an area, but besides them the Herdwicks also figure prominently in the book, as a sort of second-line corps of patriots, whose appropriateness it is more difficult to dispute inside an area marked out with so little regard for the needs o. connections of the human population.

Those who are more interested in, and familiar with, the history of the counties than the hill-rambling tourist, are less confident of the entity and homogeneity of this mystical realm. A local historian, such as the late Miss Armitt of Rydal, detected differences of dialect, social organisation, and life even between the two sides of the River Brathay. Thus in Furness were found the North Lancashire folk with their woodland crafts of charcoal-making and iron-bloomeries, whilst to the north were the sheep-farmers and the woollen trade. Obviously, valleys looking downstream to such a town as Cockermouth had little connection of any sort with those looking towards Kendal. Indeed, the fact that the Duddon valley from its head, for all civil purposes, depended on Lancaster, just as the Rothay and Brathay valleys were part of the Barony of Kendal, is eloquent enough. Until 1856 the bishopric of Carlisle did not include West Cumberland south of Workington, nor Furness, nor the half of Westmorland lying south of Shap Fells and Dunmail Raise. These areas, together including quite half of the Lake District, had belonged to the archdeaconry of Richmond. In mountain districts everywhere, the mountains divide and

M

not unite. For market, play, business, schooling, or law, the
eyes of valley-dwellers inevitably turn downstream. Mr.
Symonds himself would probably appreciate the reasons for
the head of Ennerdale being attached to the West Cumberland conurbation, and not merely part of the Wordsworth-
shire National Park, if he should have the misfortune to break
his leg there.

One must almost apologise for quoting here the oft-
quoted passage from the *Journal* of Thomas Gray's tour,
about Styhead: 'All further access is here barred to prying
mortals; only there is a little path winding over the fells, and
for some weeks in the year passable to the dalesmen. . . .'
All sorts of interpretations have been put on this passage—
the supposed unknown state of the Lake District, our
ancestors' incapacity for dealing with mountains, Gray's
personal timidity, as well as ('the mountains know well that
these innocent people will not reveal the mysteries of their
ancient kingdom') the people's interest in concealing or even
in obstructing public use of the route they used for smuggling.
This last is particularly hard to believe. Though no doubt
some traffic did come this way from that smugglers' sanctuary
the Isle of Man, it could hardly have been on so large a scale
as to support that explanation. To the end of the eighteenth
century the Solway coast was much more given to wild ways
and to smuggling than the mountain valleys. Gray's next
sentence makes it clear that at least he had been told just
where the track led. Let us suppose therefore that he meant
just a little sensational flourish, not to be taken seriously by
anyone, to round off his day in Borrowdale. The point is
that, considered as a necessary link for all civilised purposes,
and not merely as an optional promenade for tourists, the
Styhead track would have been hopelessly inadequate, and
no doubt the farmers of Seathwaite and Wasdale would meet
as often at Cockermouth as at Kern Knotts. The track
over the pass and every habitation in the neighbouring
vales were surveyed at the scale of one inch to the mile
by a private surveyor in the very next year to Gray's

visit. So much for Polite Letters as documentary evidence.

The real story of the Lake Counties can hardly be made to correspond with this. Other parts of England must be as Scandinavian as Cumbria, so many of whose place-names are Welsh, and whose shepherds till lately counted their sheep in the ancient language of the Cymry. Far from its being true that the District was never conquered by the Normans, their first wave of conquest swept over South Westmorland and Furness, whilst Malcolm of Scots seized the opportunity of the temporary dislocation of English power to re-assert his overlordship of the rest of the region. In 1092 Rufus pushed the English frontier up to Carlisle, although for many more years the country, with the rest of the North, was much subject to Scottish feudal and ecclesiastical influence, as well as military inroads, varying with the relative strengths of the two Crowns. In 1138 Ranulf of Chester, after one such interlude, again overran the fiefs which Rufus had added to England. But there is no suggestion that the mountain mass at any time played the part of a fortress-refuge of any northern Llewellyn or Hereward the Wake, or that its people were capable of significant resistance except as part of the feudal levies of the two counties. Life in the Vale of Eden or in the fertile coastal districts in mediaeval times must have called for the full development of warlike qualities. More would no doubt have been heard of the misfortunes of the mountain dalesmen if there had been more there to plunder; but they did occasionally suffer from invaders as fierce as and even more hungry than themselves. The small peletowers, though useful against roving bands of a few masterless men, could be burnt wholesale whenever there was a major expedition from Scotland, such as those of 1315 or 1322. Such as have survived are not conspicuous in the dales most familiar to tourists. The one at Kentmere lies nearer the hills than they are usually found.

The origin of the Herdwick breed of sheep is not historically clear, but they do not resemble the sheep of such isles associated with the Norsemen as the Shetlands. The Rough

Fell, Lonks, and Blackface, widely spread over the North, are much closer. Sheep-farming is more prominently associated with the Cistercians, with their great estates ruled from Holm Cultram, Calder, and Furness Abbeys (to name those in our region) than with the far-off Norsemen. It was very much an export industry, and in connection with it we hear of such things as the long strings of packhorses to London, new wealth born of keen management, the many fulling-mills and dyers, and even the beginnings of Time-and-Motion technique in the high industrial efficiency of the knitters. The wool (and the cloth) trade indeed were for many centuries a great part of our national economy, and history—matters of intensely practical concern not to be obscured by vague expressions such as 'a way of life'. Those who prefer to speak of agriculture as a way of life rather than a business, can only mean either the poorest and most primitive sorts of subsistence-farming such as have hardly been predominant anywhere in England since the Normans, or else a sheltered pretence of agriculture really dependent on the surplus profits of industry or commerce elsewhere.

Cumberland and Westmorland (and to a less degree Lancashire North of the Sands), do indeed have in common a great deal of history and tradition. It was not, however, at all centred on the mountains which have been adopted as the core of the National Park, but on the Border. Here what was significant was not so much the actual frontier, which, disputed as it was, largely took its route by quicksands, mosses, and moors, but in what we should in the last war have called a defence in depth with hedgehog positions—the larger castles down to Kendal and Lancaster, with the rich lowlands which supported them. In 1249 were codified the Border Laws, supposed to be merely a re-enactment of customs ancient even at that time, providing for the suppression of banditry by international judicial procedure. The people of the two counties likewise claimed, as an ancient right, exemption from all military service other than the convoying of the King's army from Rerecross on Stainmore

to Solway March: in the vanguard when going north and in
the rearguard when returning. Those who wrote for the
early tourists, such as Clarke (1774), do not forget to feature
these martial traditions. In the Pilgrimage of Grace in 1536,
the two counties, along with the rest of the North, rose
against religious and political innovation, but on this western
side of the Pennines the movement was one of the people,
without much participation by the local feudal leaders and
gentry. In 1577, however, in the rising of the Northern Earls,
it was Lancashire which held back, no doubt because lying
nearer the seat of government, and further from the now-
collusive Scots, it had less hope of impunity. Thereafter, a
tighter grip afforded by the presence of considerable
mercenary garrisons on the frontier, enabled Elizabeth's
government to extirpate local disaffection, so that by the
eighteenth century the Jacobite traditions which persisted
in Lancashire had no counterpart here. (The Earl of
Derwentwater indeed met with personal tragedy in 1715,
but his principal seat was in Tynedale.) Only a little later,
Thomas West, the author of the earliest local *Guide* for
tourists, ministered peaceably and undisturbed, if with
extreme discretion, as chaplain to the remnant of those of
his faith.

In the latter part of the eighteenth century took place
another movement affecting the two counties: 'The rise of a
powerful force in local politics, which for ambition and
daring has seldom been equalled, and never surpassed in the
north-west counties'. This was Sir James Lowther's attempt
to establish a sort of private dominion or special position of
influence, of which representation in the Commons, local
patronage exercised through, by, and for himself and his
partisans on behalf of the grateful government, and his
own great economic power, were to be the mutually
supporting pillars. According to the practice of the spoils-
system usual in eighteenth-century politics, this probably
seemed scarcely immoral to contemporaries, and might well
have enabled him to build up an almost unassailable local

realm within the Realm. He already controlled the votes of half a score of members of parliament, known as 'Lowther's Ninepins'. It seems that even the county boundaries played a part as one small aspect of this politico-economic game, for Hodgson's map (1771) shows 'Boundary as claimed by Sir James Lowther' and 'Boundary as claimed by Sir Henry Vane'. The critical trials of strength took place in 1768, in the Cumberland election, which cost £130,000, and in the fight in parliament over the Nullum Tempus Bill. (This Bill was an ingenious attempt, by means of general legislation, to undermine the title to land, and thus the electoral strength, of his local rivals the Bentincks.) The election contest resulted in each side getting one candidate returned; and right down to the Reform Act the parties were satisfied with a concordat on these lines.

The story of this attempt to achieve a special position of dominance by legal expedients suggests an interesting historical comparison with the successful modern agitation for the carving of a large slice of the three historic counties, and the attempt to gain control over the key function of Planning, by those who wished to make certain ideals of landscape preservation prevail over the possible opposition of the people of the area concerned. The objects of Sir James Lowther and of the Friends of the Lake District were of course entirely different, and it is not suggested that the latter were motivated by the wish for pecuniary advantage. For Sir James likewise it should be said that neither were his objectives—a two-way traffic in 'interest' or the mutual support of patron and client, so well understood in eighteenth-century England—considered immoral in his day. It may be that a similar stalemate, or, as one may care to consider it, a similar unwilled but beneficial co-operation, may be the out-come of the efforts in our own times of those who are exclusively devoted to picturesque amenity, to gain the numerical preponderance on the Park Planning Authorities which prior to the passing of the National Parks Act the Hobhouse Committee had seemed to promise them.

CHAPTER XXII

NATIONAL TRUST

THIS MOVEMENT for the preservation of natural scenery had its beginning at a time when, as it might well seem to us to-day, there was no great threat. The break-up of large estates, the building boom of the 'twenties, the grandiose frame of mind among planners of roads and so on, the heavier pressure of demand for water-supply, the world wars themselves, all were, at the end of the nineteenth century, invisibly distant in the future. What endangered picturesque and historical scenes had not hitherto been active forces so much as ignorance, indifference and neglect, coupled with the lack of any protection in law or any mobilisation of public opinion. In the last decade and a half of the nineteenth century, however, although the industrial revolution was by then a hundred years old, we do notice a certain acceleration in the tempo of life generally, of finance, of transport, and still wider extension of man's physical demands on nature. The 'eighties was the most vigorous period of railway promotion since the 'forties. Early in the 'nineties, the electric tramcar (surely the most innocent of mankind's bulkier toys) indicated at least that the urban masses were becoming mobile.

In 1894 Harcourt's new death duties, as the first deliberate attempt to redistribute wealth by means of taxation, presaged the doom of the big landowner; although the modern scale of taxation for the fantastic expenditures of war and peace had not yet crippled his power to give rein to his imagination in planning, to impose planning order on others, or to protect the amenity that existed. He might well, indeed, play the vandal himself on occasion. In the Lake District, the removal to the gardens of Lowther Castle of much of the carved stonework of Shap Abbey is an example, though atoned by much else on the same estate. But if sometimes he erred, usually he gave, so far as picturesqueness and artistic achievement were concerned, vastly more than he took away. One would hardly wish to have all the mediaeval manor-houses of England (supposing some earlier National Trust had existed for their preservation) at the price of the Renaissance or eighteenth-century mansions which have been erected on their foundations and with their materials. During the years when landowners were powerful and the wider public desiring access was small, landowners might tend to encroach on public rights, although one imagines that things more or less found their due level according to the local needs of the times. The sudden growth of urban populations, however, threw off its balance the old interplay of forces, and more rights of way and of rambling for recreational purposes were found to be needed. The earliest public efforts therefore were for securing footpaths and access to open land, rather than for preservation of scenery.

The National Trust may almost be called a Lake District institution, for its first properties were there, beginning with some woods on the west side of Derwentwater in 1901. The Trust has of course no compulsory powers nor, strictly, public functions—it is simply a landholding body—but was able to serve as a rallying-point for public feeling. The responsibilities of its position as a landowner, the widely differing characters of the properties it held, and, one may add, the differing points of view of its supporters, have limited its indulgence in opinionative propaganda. Nevertheless, the aggregate of its efforts in particular cases amounted indirectly to a second main function: that of educating the public at large to value the treasures of scenery, architecture, and historical interest it made accessible to them.

Under the warm enthusiastic guidance of a Rawnsley, the early days of the Trust were a halcyon time in which it must have seemed unnecessary to contemplate the questions of principle and problems of administration which its later growth brought into view. In those early days each small acquisition seemed to be an offering at the shrine of Beauty herself; not measured by its relation to any master plan for the district, but as a testimony of allegiance to the ultimate principle (the details left in pious confidence to be worked out later) of a Britain visibly expressing, in the management of her land and in her care for the relics of her past, a sound attitude to tradition, to aesthetics, to work and to play. The properties acquired included those accepted and held expressly 'for preservation,' as well as those not under such a restriction. They came to include famous viewpoints where the essential purpose was to secure public access, as well as large areas of other land where public access would have been incompatible with use for agriculture, or which were only required to prevent damage to adjacent beauty-spots. Just as many ancient houses were donated to secure their preservation for future generations as architectural masterpieces, yet continued to be privately occupied, so also woods, farms, and even moors could be accepted for the preservation of their general character and place in the landscape, whilst the sporting and fishing rights continued to be let. The countryside, in fact, was considered as a living organism, not merely as a fairground exhibit.

With the steady growth in the National Trust's properties, the donation of new ones came to have rather less the character of a romantic gesture in favour of Beauty Imprisoned in the Attic, and questions of policy and management began to loom larger. The extent to which such problems were for a long time solved, with no other policy than reliance on tradition and on discretion, arouses admiration. Tradition, indeed, has been much less of a force in the Lake District than some visitors might choose to think it. Such singularity as its domestic architecture has retained has been the result of necessity rather than deliberate choice. Much of the attraction of the district depends on the individuality dictated by the rocky unyielding materials of its landscape, unfriendly to large-scale enterprise or planning or elaborate craftsmanship.

The National Trust's empire in the Lake District nowadays consists of more than 30,000 acres in ownership, with
another 14,000 under restrictive covenant, as well as a voice
in the control of some 50,000 acres of common-land. For a
concern such as this, it becomes increasingly difficult to base
a policy merely on tradition, discretion, harmony with
existing development, and so on—if only because the Trust
itself is or looks like becoming the biggest fish in the pond.
Even a tradition may develop, and alter, but a tradition
which has grown naturally out of small-scale peasant free-
hold ownership is no longer organic when the attempt is
made by a great and centralised corporate body to administer it for the novel purposes of picturesqueness or the
comfort of tourists. It is not a question of going slowly, or of
care in patching the new to resemble the old—the thing has
to this extent lost its meaning and become impossible: one
cannot become a sycophant to oneself. In the future, therefore, if for this reason alone, it will surely become necessary
for the National Trust to work out a positive picturesqueness,
or positive beauty policy of its own, free from reliance on
the sentiment attaching to the rustic England of the mid-
nineteenth century, or any other 'period'.

It is possible thus to regret that so great a proportion of
a countryside should come under one landlord, however
competent and sympathetic. The mistakes of the individual
owner are the condition of vitality. The opposite danger is
that of Ghastly Good Taste. Nothing in the irregular charm
of the old Lakeland village was or can in the future be the
creation of the large-scale corporate landlord, however
myopic the spectacles he may choose to wear.

The sense of isolation, individuality, and seclusion of the
kind provided by the irregularly built cottages and inaccessible valleys of the Lake District, which so strongly
appealed to the later Victorians and to the Edwardians—in
fact to guilt-ridden escapists from Wordsworth down—can
hardly retain its reality under even the most enlightened
management from Grosvenor Gardens. It is easy to preserve

walls and buildings, quite a different matter to preserve an atmosphere, at least a genuine atmosphere. But the desire for this particular sort of thing is perhaps already dated, and the town-dwellers of tomorrow may demand from their National Park something quite different.

A danger of another sort is illustrated by the case of Wray Castle, by the shore of Windermere. This building was, in its origin (about 1840) one of the more expensive flights of the romantic fancy. Besides the mock-mediaeval, there were fake ruins of two different 'periods'. No doubt in its earlier days Wray incurred a certain amount of safe disapproval from the timid, just as in later times it was an easy target for the epithet of Victorian. None the less, it succeeded in working its passage, as it was intended to do, as an element in a picturesque landscape. It always figured frequently in illustrations of the district, and in its later days, came to have an additional interest as a monument of a certain period of taste. It is not a question whether one admires it or not, any more than one need admire (as a piece of design) a particular example of a 'traditional' farmhouse. The time came, however, when the needs of the mansion's tenants (a scientific institution) required its extension, and it would have been necessary to carry this out in a somewhat different style. The only answer which could be given by the Trust in pursuance of a policy of offending nobody was 'No'. Accordingly, the building ceased to be suitable for the purposes of its tenants, and it seems more than probable it will become completely derelict. This seems not unlikely to typify the fate of the district as a whole, and its human concerns, great and small, under the best-intentioned policy of mere 'preservation'.*

The proper function of the National Trust in an area, once a National Park has been established, is another problem. There seems little doubt that there is no need for the Trust to keep on acquiring the ownership of large areas of typical

---

* As the book goes to print I am glad to record that Wray seems likely, after many years, again to find occupants.

property, or even restrictive covenants, merely to ensure its proper planning, for public authority has ample powers to see to this. Mr. B. L. Thompson, then the National Trust's representative in the North of England, said in *The National Trust and the Lake District* (1945) that if a National Park were established there

the National Trust's need to extend its properties would presumably cease within the National Park area because all problems of preservation and access would be settled by the National Park Commissioners. On the other hand the Trust would be able to devote itself much more intensely to the peculiarly interesting and important work of preserving and improving the very considerable estates for which it had become responsible, and thus showing how trusteeship can be at once conservative and progressive. The Trust's properties would become 'models of good taste and good management, skilfully combining the practical with some element of poetry'.

We may go a little further, and envisage the Trust acquiring a few additional properties of special character, such as mansions containing valuable pictures or furniture, or gardens, in the case of which specially skilled management would be required. This would not be the case with mere farm-land, woodland or 'rough' ground, unless it was thought possible thereby to give the opportunity for some model, or especially some experimental, standard of management. This latter aim might perhaps be better effected by an *ad hoc* arrangement or through a smaller body, and should preferably be limited in duration, in order that the administrative set-up might not outlast the inspiration or leadership.

Mr. Hugh Dalton, when Chancellor of the Exchequer in 1946, took a different view, probably in pursuance of a belief that public ownership was a good thing in itself, in any event, whether inside or outside National Parks. In that year he established the National Land Fund of fifty million pounds, the interest on which was to be used for purchasing properties the owners of which were prepared to sell them in satisfaction of death duties. These properties might then be handed on by the Treasury to the National Trust, or in some cases to other organisations such as the Youth Hostels

Association. This scheme temporarily ceased to be actively operated in 1954. One may be glad that this is so (although it is not possible to say what future policy may be) since the effect of giving land to the National Trust wholesale must be to overload the Trust's administrative organisation, thereby dehumanising it and making it far too like a branch of the Civil Service or of nationalised industry. Such an indiscriminately swollen body would less easily bring the special care, taste, and knowledge to properties of a special character which should in the future be the particular justification for the existence of the Trust. It would be as if the Tal-y-llyn Railway (well-known indirectly to admirers of Mr. Emmet's work) were to fall into the hands of the British Transport Commission.

Where highly specialised expertise is the requirement, a vast undertaking does of course have a great advantage, and can deploy this advantage at least in cases lucky enough to attract the attention and approval of its policy-makers at headquarters. The restoration of ancient pictures, buildings, and other fabrics is an example. Where, however, the encouragement of a living tradition is at issue, or where it is a question of creative or imaginative qualities, or of safeguarding what Wordsworth called 'minute possibilities of beauty', the advantage of a large organisation is by no means obvious. Such a body cannot and will not so readily avail itself of the zeal or knowledge of the local public, or of interested scholars or artists (or even mere enthusiasts) who do not happen to be professional administrators. In this connection, the gradual submergence of the local managing committees (often representative of those to whose enthusiasm the acquisition of properties was due) is to be deplored. Perhaps the loss is, above all, one of diversity of thought. But diversity is one of the charms of Lakeland. The Trust would no doubt deny, and indeed has denied, that the extinction or nullification of these local committees is its policy. Whether practice has conformed to this expression of policy is another matter.

The loss of touch with local life which is involved when a property is accepted for preservation in perpetuity by a corporate landlord, or when that landlord is no longer willing to be troubled with the smaller local committees of management, appears perhaps an insignificant matter in the case of any one property. In many cases, no doubt, an active and efficient agent of the Trust may succeed a private owner who is an absentee, old, poor, or a mere trustee. But in the aggregate, the growth of too great a domain in the hands of the Trust could be a burden on the political and spiritual life of the community in much the same way as a great private estate sometimes was, antipathetic to change and spontaneity, and lying as a heavy mortmain hand on the feeble beginnings of new movements. In any case, the Lake District was always traditionally the home of the *independent* occupier, the 'estatesman', and there can be little doubt of the mark which this independence and small-scale ownership, whatever its inconveniences, has left on the local character. Even general nationalisation would not have this disadvantage, for then control would be democratic at the centre, even if not locally. (Which, reader, would you take, if you had the choice of central or of local democracy?) The Trust, operating from a headquarters in the metropolis, numbering among its supporters many people influential in departments unconnected with rural or local life, and speaking *ex officio* in the name of the Good and the Beautiful, can, and even now does, exert more effective influence at all governmental levels than a merely landholding body, concerned with its own properties, and has more means of influence at its disposal, in propaganda, and in headquarters contacts, than any locally elected authority. Its views, expressed at local enquiries or to the National Parks Commission, must deeply and widely affect the life of the whole Cumbrian area. One may instance such questions as road policy (and consequently transport and village welfare dependent thereon), the siting and design of buildings for all the purposes of life, commons, the means for electricity distribution, use of natural resources in the national economic interest, industry and land use of all kinds. I do not seek here to discuss whether the Trust's influence has been wrongly used. Illiberal influences undoubtedly exist in its counsels, as for example the noble lord, a member of its central executive Committee, who, apropos of a matter on which his opinion had failed very narrowly to prevail on that Committee, remarked to myself: 'I would rather see the people of ****** all under the sod, than have ****** spoiled.' Let credit go where credit is due, and much is due to National Trust management. But if the Trust is to be allowed to grow any larger, and to enjoy respect as a semi-public body, some way must be found of associating it once more with the life of the areas in which its influence is great. This is not to say that local influence should be predominant, but that actual responsibility for Trust policies should be known, and means should be found for the *open* expression in its counsels, of public opinion, perhaps by the appointment of some members of its advisory committees, by the elective local authority. At present the Trust's own members are for practical purposes as powerless and as much in the dark as anyone else about what really happens, between the lines of its agreeably produced and reassuringly written annual reports. In conclusion, I would like to rebut the charge that I am wantonly or perversely attacking a well-meaning set of people who have so far achieved so much to the general satisfaction. There is no need for me to heap easy flattery on an organisation which is well able to attend to its own propaganda. My task is to supply criticism which may help it to avoid dangers and attune itself better still to the needs of the future.

CHAPTER XXIII

THE AGE OF BLUE BOOKS

THE PERIOD of all this propagandist activity was naturally followed by one in which the picturesqueness of the Lake District and the means to be taken for its defence became the subject of political and parliamentary action. The progress of debate and of subsequent administrative action, interesting as they are in themselves, are not however the theme of this book.

In 1929 Mr. Ramsay Macdonald, at the head of a minority government, had found it appropriate to raise the question of National Parks. This was in harmony with left-wing principle and the wish to do something to make England a land fit for her heroes to live in, yet was also attractive in its practical aspect to many more or less right-wing people; and so might be hoped to be innocuous, from a party point of view. He appointed a Committee under the chairmanship of Dr. Christopher Addison to investigate, and this reported in 1931. Its recommendations were that a National Parks Commission should be established, which should offer guidance to local authorities in the exercise of their planning powers, and should help to co-ordinate joint action by them in the areas suitable for national parks. At this date the function of planning was entrusted, not to counties, but to the lesser local government areas, and the expression 'national' merely denoted the national sponsorship necessary for parks too extensive for a single local authority to establish, and did not have the esoteric meaning which was later attached to it. It was further intended that the proposed Commission was to consult with and to examine the proposals of government departments and large statutory bodies which might affect park areas. Such proposals included artillery ranges, water-power schemes, cable lines and afforestation, matters which in very many cases were (especially at that date) entirely outside the consideration of planning authorities. The Commission was also to have the duties of allocating government grants, developing policy and recommending it to public opinion; but it was not contemplated that it should supersede the elected authorities, whether of county or district, in any of their functions.

The Addison Committee's report, appearing in 1931, fell on the stony ground of the great financial depression, so that no immediate action was taken on it; but it served just as effectively in the end, as a *point d'appui* for the efforts to form public opinion, which continued throughout the 'thirties.

A further decisive push came at a time when it might not have been anticipated. The Access to Mountains Act 1939 had been ineffective in practice and disappointing to its advocates. In the Lake District, of course, access to mountains had never been a problem at all. But, comparatively early in World War II, people's minds began to turn idealistically towards the changes to be made when it should end, and in October 1941 Lord Reith, then Minister of Works and Buildings, in consultation with the Ministry of Agriculture appointed a departmental committee to consider the post-war use of land in rural areas for purposes of industry and construction. This committee, which was under the chairmanship of Lord Justice Scott, reported in 1942. Although the Lake District is hardly mentioned specifically, the Report is an important link in the development of the ideas in which we are interested, and its sentiment and tone are very much those of professed lovers of the Lake District. The full terms of reference were:

To consider the conditions which should govern building and other constructional development in country areas—consistently with the maintenance of agriculture, and, in particular, the factors affecting the location of industry, having regard to:

> economic operation
> part-time and seasonal employment
> the well-being of rural communities and
> the preservation of rural amenities.

N

It is arguable that these instructions were directed to the perfectly prosaic and obvious problems of industrial development which would face the country after the war—with only a minimum of heightened sensibility about the social and aesthetic aspects. On any showing, one must admire, in those times, a certain degree of faith in the future, although one may doubt whether the time was really favourable for the exercise of prophecy. It is mainly during the early stages— say one-third of the way through—a war or a revolution, before the maximum effort has developed, that such musings have their attraction. At such a time, planning for the peace is a way of reassuring oneself, filling up the time of anticlimax when morale might otherwise sink. But as a struggle for survival, war must frequently transform the familiar world beyond expectation, and must reach a stage when the modes of continued existence are shaped by necessity, rather than by the book. After it is over, things get themselves re-fashioned as available skills and pressures permit, not in obedience to slogans dating from before the crisis.

Whilst noticing the particular bias of the Committee, one need not go so far as to accuse them of going beyond their terms of reference. Where the Minister might have had in mind the future of industrial construction, with due regard to its spatial and social repercussions, the Committee had before its eyes the shining vision yclept The English Countryside, and the dangers threatening it by reason of social or aesthetic Sin. 'We are united,' they write, 'in sharing a deep love for our countryside', and then comes a long quotation, by which they clearly intend to strike the keynote of their Report which follows:

There is no countryside like the English countryside for those who have learned to love it; its firm yet gentle lines of hill and dale, its ordered confusion of features, its hamlets and old churches, its farms and ricks and great barns and ancient trees, its pools and ponds and shining threads of rivers, its flower-starred hedgerows, its orchards and woodland patches, its village greens and kindly inns. . . . Other countrysides have their pleasant aspects, but none such variety, none that shine so steadfastly throughout the year. . . . None change scene and character in three miles of walking, nor have so mellow a sunlight nor so diversified a cloudland nor confess the perpetual refreshment of the strong soft winds that blow off the sea, as our mother England does.

This passage, to which such prominence was given, was from the works of Mr. H. G. Wells, and its sentiments reflect the emotional history of his contemporaries. When he began to write, around the beginning of this century, mechanism and industry were still rising stars—the aeroplane a hopeful toy, the by-law street layout and the tramcar signs of progress, the prosperity of Britain's coal and cotton assured. But, since these halcyon days, the first world war, the excesses of the 'twenties and the depression of the early 'thirties, had markedly lowered the prestige, if not of mechanisation itself, at least of industrial leadership and the towns it had created. Romance now no longer brought up the nine-fifteen. Well before the second world war, men wished to think of 'the countryside' as a place of stable and unquestioned values, an abiding refuge, most of all from the world which they themselves had made and in which they continued to spend their normal lives. The changes in Wells' own tone during his life skilfully reflected the changing yearnings of his contemporaries. The quotation's somewhat facile style has been much imitated since, and it is not altogether his fault if it now sounds to us like an advertisement for beer.

In reading the Report, we frequently become aware that the 'rural amenities' and 'rural communities' which appear in the terms of reference are to the majority of the committee something more than just the actual communities or amenities which would be noticed by an objective observer, outside the main concentrations of population. They are amenities and communities inherently rural, after a master-pattern laid up in heaven; like that of the ancient Merrie England, which was much merrier than England ever was in cold fact. The organisation of such a village is affectionately described. By coincidence, it is romantically placed, like Sir Walter Scott's *Waverley*, 'sixty years ago'. Economically it must be based on farming if it is to retain

those features which give it distinctive charm and character
—this, in the Committee's words, is their 'basic assumption'.
The bases of this assumption are not submitted to examina-
tion by them, as they recognise that the details of farming
and of agricultural policy are outside their terms of reference.
In one place in their report they do indeed appear to be
aware that farming methods and objects have profoundly
changed 'even within the last hundred years'.

It would be unfair to the Committee to imply that improvements on the ancient pattern were not contemplated.
In many places they express warm hopes that housing will
improve, that parish councils will do their duty, that rural
justices will discourage 'the abuses which have come to be
associated with the term "road house"' where such premises
are near villages, that land will not go out of cultivation, and
so on. All this is to happen by unexplained means, or to be
imposed from above. But village life is to be kept uncon-
taminated by town influences except where some strong
particular reason of policy exists for running the risk. So
tender are the Committee of their ideal, that they actually
recommend that noxious industrial vapours should not be
released in the countryside. One is left to suppose that they
prefer them released in the more thickly populated centres.

Townsmen, it seems as one reads the Report, do not
become rural merely by living, at their own wish, away from
towns; their warrant for doing so rests on nothing better
than individualistic preference, itself (in the same Wellsian
way of thinking) more than half discredited. If the right of
the 'townsman' to settle in the countryside is thus challenged,
the latter, purged and 'preserved', is to become part of the
'heritage' of townsmen collectively. The development to be
admitted is not to be free development, not development
resulting from demand, least of all individual demand, and
not in any event the assimilation of town and country
dwellers.

It is hardly surprising, therefore, that the Committee
should sense with uneasiness 'a degree of misunderstanding,

even of antagonism, between townsman and countryman'
even if they are wrong in placing this as something which
'remained at the outbreak of the war' and not as the likely
consequence of their own proposed division of the English
people into two distinct castes, of unequal size and privileges.
'There is much to be done,' they say, 'to create the mutual
understanding and sympathy that are necessary if all sections
of the community are to enjoy the countryside which, if it is
the heritage of all, is in the guardianship of the countryman.'
If this reflection had really been, like some Sleeping Beauty,
awaiting original discovery by the Committee, one might
well ask what the English people had been doing throughout
all their history, since Dick Whittington first went up to
London to make his fortune, or Jack of Newbury began
organising the textile industry in Wessex villages in the
fifteenth century.

Words like 'townsman', 'heritage' and 'countryside', placed,
as we have occasionally placed them, within quotation
marks, represent the special meanings with heavy overtones
of which one is so conscious in reading the Report, and will
be felt to have attached to them a strong flavour of their
period. This preference for fixed categories independent of
observed fact, and with strong emotional associations,
betrays the essentially literary (rather than practical or
statistical) character of the Committee's vision. Much in
their Report may be considered as a late flowering, watered
by the steady stream of propaganda in the preceding decade,
of the ideas put into currency by romantic novelists from the
beginning of the century, rather than of the somewhat
puritanical and anti-escapist feeling characteristic of the
'thirties period itself. Where such a foundation of suggestion
is laid, over a long period, slight though the immediate
impression may seem, the strength and toughness of the
popular mystique deriving therefrom may ultimately be
found to be enormous.

CHAPTER XXIV

THE PHILOSOPHER KINGS

AT THE END OF THE WAR, the Government being now persuaded of the desirability of National Parks, the next step was to commission Mr. John Dower, an architect, to 'study the question further' and in effect to prepare a brief, of which the Minister could avail himself if he chose. This decision to appoint an individual marks the end of the merely exploratory stage and a resolve to proceed to practical planning. Dower was himself a convinced and close associate of what had come to be known as 'the amenity group', the policy of which had been evolved in the circle of the Councils for the Preservation of Rural England (founded in 1926) and of Rural Wales. Dower was not the man to lapse into the occasional infantilisms of a heterogeneous committee. His brilliant paper was comprehensive, tactful, and persuasive; but these qualities should not obscure for us the intransigence of its basic points of view. I do not suggest that he in any way improperly disguised these; but so wise a man as he does not, for example, make a frontal attack on such a leviathan as democratic local government, thickly armoured in its statutory authority, tradition, and vested interest, by discharging a squib in its face; nor, if resolved upon such an undertaking as revolutionising the recreational tastes of the mass of the people, does he throw in all his forces at the outset. Criticism of these tastes is none the less strongly implied in the Report and indeed often frankly emerges. 'In practice, it will be by no means easy for the National Parks authority to resist the inevitable demand of the urban-holiday-minded that they should have their share in the National Parks programme. . . . As the number of visitors increases, it will not be possible or desirable to exclude altogether some development of facilities for their indoor entertainment and

for ball-games or some more concentrated forms of outdoor
recreation. . . . But all such things should be permitted only
after the most careful scrutiny both of themselves and of
their likely consequences.' Thus, we fear, speaks a tyrant in
embryo, albeit a tyrant after the pattern of Plato's philosopher kings.

Dower was not the only begetter of the National Park idea
nor its principal champion, but we may fairly take him as
its standard-bearer as it existed in 1945, occupying the midway position in the front line of its embattled array, to which
it was his task to give coherence. Let us look at the movement
as it appears from his pages at that time. His carefully
considered statement of what a National Park is, runs as
follows:

> An extensive area of beautiful and relatively wild country, in which—
> for the nation's benefit, and by appropriate national decision and
> action—
> The characteristic landscape beauty is strictly preserved—
> Access and facilities for open-air enjoyment are provided—
> Wild life, and buildings and places of architectural and historic
>   interest are preserved—
> The established farming is suitably maintained.

We do not wish to read the Report unsympathetically, or to
pick out weaknesses of detail, if there are any. In a great
movement, there are bound to be cases in which a wrong
road is temporarily followed, and is afterwards retraced;
there are bound to be faults in prediction, particularly
quantitative ones. What we seek to do, therefore, is to discern
broadly and imaginatively the springs of the movement and
its relation to the contemporary climate of ideas.

Dower's forecast of such matters as the size of the National
Park areas to be created and the numbers of visitors to them
are still of interest, since they indicate not only the size but
the *sort* of thing he and those who thought like him had in
mind, and its place in the national life. Of the 58,000 square
miles in England and Wales, one-fifth were, in his words,
'relatively wild'. Disregarding the portions he considered

unsuitable for National Parks or was prepared to resign to other interests, he regarded 8000 square miles, or one-seventh of the country as potential National Parks. The whole of this potential area, and not merely the portions which it was financially and administratively possible to embody in National Parks for the time being, should be kept under the watchful eye of the National Parks Commission as a National Park Reserve, and within it no substantial development, other than for agriculture or forestry, should *prima facie* be considered desirable.

Statutory power already existed to enforce a good standard of planning over the country as a whole, and at the time Dower reported, most active and weighty consideration was being given to the renewal and extension of these powers, soon afterwards renewed and extended by the Town and Country Planning Act of 1947.

An essential characteristic of National Parks, thought Dower, was that they should not be formed or administered by the local (including county) authorities, to which normal planning functions had always been entrusted by Parliament.

Local action, even if it made consistently full and proper use of available powers, could never of its nature provide *national* parks. It might well provide a number of local parks, or by joint action, regional parks, and it is conceivable, that such a provision might, in time, be made on so considerable a scale as to leave no sufficiently clear field for national action. But the result would inevitably be local and piecemeal in character; the essential elements of national decision, national choice, and national responsibility would be lacking; and a unique opportunity would have been missed of stimulating the best kinds of open-air recreation. . . .

This is really rather high-flying doctrine. The efforts of county or even smaller authorities are apparently thought adequate to take measures against the spread of smallpox, to control police forces, to provide highways and to arrange for them to link up with those of neighbouring areas, not to speak of administering public education; all these things in a way consistent with 'national decision, national choice, and national responsibility'. But apparently not to have the planning control of areas of fell-land. Why should a system which is thought adequate to hold the balance between all the relevant claims to use of land, as for example those of industry, farming, defence, health, and communications in Britain as a whole, not have been thought adequate to protect the single issue of amenity in districts where, because of their relative wildness, the pressure and tempo of change would in any case be so much less than elsewhere? It would seem difficult to cast doubt on the ability or willingness of the ordinary planning agencies to perform this duty, without making a mock of the whole national set-up for all other planning purposes. The Lake District contains many man-made features which, separately, can be criticised on the lines of one or another aesthetic argument, or else as being out of keeping with the supposed characteristics of the district. Apart from the modern roads which bring the tourists there, the railway Wordsworth deplored, the tourists themselves, and the whole mass of mediocre architecture erected for their accommodation, one can think of such things as Penruddock limeworks, Calgarth factory, Tilberthwaite quarries, and of many other copper and lead mines, quarries, and afforestation schemes. But imagine all these absent, in a conjectural restoration, let us say, of the state of affairs at the beginning of the nineteenth century. (I had almost said: a restoration of the times of Thomas Gray and William Wordsworth. But this would be to slip too lazily into the practice, so convenient for the cultivated reader, of seeing physical and human phenomena through the eyes exclusively of literary artists. No one would claim Gray as a very keen-sighted or single-minded observer of social conditions. Poor housing may have played a part in the death of more than one of Wordsworth's own children.) If none of the unaesthetic developments above-mentioned, or others similar, had ever taken place, since the end of the eighteenth century, and the stimulus and the opportunities for variety of occupation and for advancement and growth of population which they have afforded had never been available, would not the perfectly preserved Lake District by now present a national social problem comparable with that which the 'poor white' districts of the Appalachians or the Deep South once did? Would not the snowball-like momentum of opinion and the vested accretion of sentiment now at the service of 'preservation' perhaps have been diverted in a different direction? And might not such a district anyway be really rather dull for the holiday-maker who did not happen to be a poet-mystic on the run from revolution, love, or the life of his time?

What support therefore did the National Park party propose to enlist in the running of the districts given over to their charge? In the main, Dower's Report fully endorses the sheep-farming predilections of the Reverend Mr. Symonds as well as the doctrine of the Scott Committee that farming should be expected to be at one and the same time picturesque, efficient and traditional. Unless farming could be to a certain extent efficient in the National Parks, the movement was clearly inviting heavy criticism, to be avoided if possible. Characteristically, therefore, the Report concedes that 'it must be given generous scope for changes in method and intensity of cultivation, cropping and stocking'—everything, almost, except freedom to put progressive farming first as an object in itself. Characteristically, too, the note of caution is sounded immediately after: 'This does not imply that the National Park Authority, though closely concerned, should itself be responsible for the necessary measures of economic organisation and technical direction.' The conception is rather that of one's great-aunt, a lady of unimpeachable authority in matters of morals and good taste, sitting in the background expressing the wish that one will enjoy oneself heartily, but not too boisterously, whilst naturally disclaiming any responsibility for the expenses of the party. Besides, Dower himself rather liked ordinary good farming—'a personal, though widely-shared opinion'. He was an admirer (strangely enough on aesthetic grounds) of scientific grassland improvement rather than of bracken, rushes and thorn-scrub. Lovers of genuine wildness in land-scape may perhaps feel that he thereby shows a weaker side when he goes on to say that certain parts of the country . . . 'where neither ploughing nor tidying-up was much in evidence, had a distinctly *neglected and desolate appearance*'.

So important was it to be able to point to a solid, if small, body of local support, that he goes further in conciliation towards the farmer of 'marginal' land (that is to say, land of doubtful economic value) than towards any other interest not already disposed to be an ally—proposing in the midst of his official paper what amounts to a suggestion of horse-trading:

'There will have to be a certain amount of "give and take" between farming and national park interests. . . . The (Park) Authority must be the farmer's, especially the hill-farmer's friend, giving continuous support to their legitimate claims and interests with central and local government bodies.'

Whilst making it clear that the absolute primacy of the proposed park authorities must be recognised, within their huge fiefs, Dower was willing to extend a statesmanlike hand to various interests, even to the local authorities and to government agencies with their own tasks, who might be prepared to carry out some part of the donkey work. The partisans of Nature Reserves, in particular, were given clearly to understand that they must not cherish ambitions of independence. If the docile co-operation of other agencies, private and public, could be secured, funds would obviously go further, and more and bigger National Parks could be secured. But Beauty would brook no rival. Dower was, how-ever (in contrast to the pontifical excommunication, which some others wished to apply to forestry in the Lake District), prepared to encourage the Forestry Commission to persevere, at least in well-doing, within National Parks in general, and indeed even to share out with it, in independent command, the relatively wild country. But the 'National Forest Parks' which the Forestry Commission had somewhat pre-sumptuously put forward as a substitute for the genuine article, were rejected on the ground that, in them, recreational use and landscape preservation were merely offered incidentally, and not as a dominant purpose. The god of picturesque amenity is not thus mocked. The use of land for growing trees was not considered to have the same quasi-sacramental and aesthetic value as its use, even artificially re-seeded and 'improved' as a sheep run. Only the department having the custodianship of ancient monuments was Dower, an architect himself, prepared to salute as equal and autonomous.

The association of antiquarian interests, and even perhaps of architectural and artistic interests as such, with the conception of National Park areas, is due mainly to somewhat accidental causes. Because of their relatively wild character, such areas are likely, as he saw, to contain far fewer buildings of artistic value, and rather fewer too of historical interest, than the national average. Decisive battles and sieges, for instance, commonly occur in plains, not among remote mountains. In spite of ample inducement from their leadership, it is very doubtful whether the modern ramblers or out-of-door types for whom National Parks were intended by Dower, feel any stronger interest in architecture or art than does the ordinary man in the street—one might be tempted to say less, if it were possible. Perhaps when on holiday we are in a somewhat more receptive mood towards cultural influences generally, much as we may be for that matter towards a variety of pastimes. Probably such interests really represent a legacy from the cultivated few such as those who supported the National Trust in its early days, who in turn derived them directly from Ruskin in his capacity of the last of the polymathic dilettanti. Time had been once, when the serious scholar (amateur though he might be) had both the possibility and the duty of including *everything* in his field of observation: dicotyledons and druids, armorial bearings and agricultural improvements, archaeology and artisanry. But appreciation became a tourist habit, until now the Middle Ages must be firmly associated, in the minds of many people, with closely clipped greensward, ticket offices, and the sale of picture postcards. Some revaluation might perhaps be not unwholesome—if indeed it has not already come about.

An innocent error of expectation in the Dower Report was regarding the likely extent of public response to the provision of National Parks. There seemed to be a widespread anticipation that, on the putting into effect of the administrative plans proposed for the Parks, a vast army of the public would pour through the gates to seek the approved delights in the manner laid down for them. Dower feared

that the concentration of visitors, attracted by the publicity accompanying their establishment, will lead to the most serious consequences:— damage to amenities, and overloading of facilities . . . the demand for genuinely country holidays has grown enormously and will continue to grow. It is voiced by thousands, and it reflects the more or less conscious desire of hundreds of thousands, perhaps millions more.

Not that he took a wholly illiberal view of the inrush:

Some things the visiting public might wish to do in National Parks and some of the more urban and mechanical facilities they ask for will have to be prohibited. . . . On the other hand there will have to be, from place to place, some sacrifice of those scenic delicacies which are only possible 'among the untrodden ways' and of the completely peaceful seclusion which cannot be enjoyed by more than a very few at a time.

He surely need not have worried. The holiday industries are extremely competitive, and, for generations past, have been trying what publicity and keen service can do; the public has strong and settled ideas about what it wants to do with its leisure; and it would take a good deal more than one Act of Parliament dealing with the subject of Planning, plus a year or two's administrative activity under it, to make a sizeable dent in that pattern. Not the most wholehearted appeal could quickly divert such a stream, still less an invitation qualified by chilly reserve towards the motorist, and towards 'those who wish to take their holidays gregariously and to enjoy the facilities . . . of cinemas, music halls, dance cafés, bathing pools, pleasure parks, proms, shopping centres, and the like'. For these, Dower recognised, 'National Parks are not the place. They had far better keep away, and . . . pretty certainly they will keep away, provided that any proposals to establish, within National Parks, the kind of facilities they desire, are firmly resisted.' Such was to be the shape of things to come, over massive areas aggregating the size of half a score of counties.

On the other hand, the type of holiday-maker inclined to the pursuits encouraged by Authority might to a very large extent continue to seek them outside National Parks. The naturalist might find devastated sites more interesting than moorland, the Betjemanite might prowl around the back streets of third-rate towns, the yachtsman afford to be indifferent to the notions of longshore idealists, and the lover of England, her life and her genius prefer to seek it where it is authentic rather than synthetic, viable rather than in need of preservation. The devotee of solitude, hardship, and adventure would certainly reply to the best-meant efforts of cultivated bureaucrats with a rude raspberry. So too the creative artist. So far from the anticipated rush having taken place, it is doubtful if it can be said, after several years of work by the National Park authorities, that they have been successful in attracting any greater number of visitors than would have come thither in any event.

Why then did Dower and his contemporaries expect that the masses would stampede to the National Parks on their establishment? Of course, it was anybody's guess what the prevailing mood of after-the-war would be. If the many confirmed city-dwellers who were evacuated have not shown an overwhelming wish to revisit the scenes of their interlude of simple living, or if the open-air lore willy-nilly imbibed in wartime by so many of their menfolk has not been developed in the direction of approved National Park pursuits, the mistake is pardonable. These upheavals have indeed had their effect, but Dower's main reasons lie much farther back in the history of the movement.

In 1937 Professor G. M. Trevelyan had said: 'It is not a question of physical exercise only, it is a question of spiritual exercise and enjoyment. . . .' Then follow some striking words, which we italicise:—

The condition of any real value in modern city life is holidays spent in the country. Natural beauty . . . alone makes a common appeal to the sectaries of all our religious creeds, to the lovers of all our different schools of poetry and art . . . it is the highest common denominator in the spiritual life of to-day.

He went on to add that until the end of the eighteenth century, the works of man only added to the beauty of nature, a doctrine so surprising that one would have been glad to have a little more documentation of it, coming as it did from an eminent historian. The gist of all this seems to be a despair of the whole of modern life; after reading Dower one understands that this despair extends not merely to the urban workshops the present-day English live in because they must, but also to their civic projects, to what they choose to make of their living quarters, and to what they do with their leisure.

With this kind of pronouncement, we enter a field of mystical values, quite remote from the everyday atmosphere of democratic compromise and practical considerations in which most of our other public affairs are conducted. Trevelyan's remarks do not of course stand alone—one continually meets their like, particularly in the sector of National Park propaganda concerned with the Lake District. In reading the apologias for religious belief, one is familiar with a similar experience; all is plain sailing and closely-knitted reasonableness, until one suddenly realises that one is being invited to pass in one blind step over the gulf which unassisted reason does not bridge. One can now understand why the amenity school did not favour the administration of park areas by existing authorities. What they sought to create was something not quite of this world, in a Cause which like Juggernaut's chariot must never be allowed to retreat before the unbeliever. This was sought (not very honestly) to be disguised by the persistent association of the label 'national' in connection with the movement for scenic parks, so that as a matter of common speech it is difficult now not to use the two words together. But indeed (as Lord Silkin remarked) the true antithesis is not, as was claimed, between 'local interests' and 'amenity', but between 'amenity' and all the rest of true national interests. In this sort of writing it becomes necessary to recognise the pass-words, the formulas expressive of dogma, which are apt to mean rather more than they say, and whose strongest support is in some underlying feeling of mystical character. For 'national' in this sense one should read, perhaps, 'authoritarian'? Clearly, to the zealot, no workaday elected body, or department of government, no jury of his fellow-countrymen, could be allowed to arbitrate, when the Cause should come into conflict with other needs.

CHAPTER XXV

THE NATIONAL PARKS ACT

HAVING THUS pulled the subject together by focussing it in the mind of an individual of strong convictions, the Minister (Mr. Silkin) now appointed another Committee, naturally chosen in the main from those in sympathy with the policy which he had already decided to implement, to comb it over once again. Sir Arthur Hobhouse was chairman, and Dower a member. Their instructions were to consider Dower's Report and to make recommendations as to the areas to be selected and the administrative measures necessary to carry the determined policy into action. Their Report is not therefore the place in which we should expect to find many important novel ideas. But as the product of their labours was a set of proposals in a more or less practical form, the Hobhouse Report served, from its appearance in 1947 until Parliament had adjudicated upon the matter (and even after that time) as a rallying-point or war-cry. It only remains for us to look at one or two ways in which it extends, or diverges from, Dower's.

The Committee dealt with the first part of their task by recommending the selection as Parks of some 5632 square miles, or just ten per cent. of the area of England and Wales, including a Lake District Park of 892 square miles. In Park areas, farming and essential rural interests were to be encouraged, but other development to be permitted only as a privilege, and therefore subject to such conditions as might be imposed, without calling for compensation. Large-scale forms of land use, such as water catchment, mining and quarrying, military training and forestry, were to be permitted only upon proved national necessity. The policy of land-purchase by Government agencies in National Park areas was endorsed—as a working hypothesis it was estimated

o

that ten per cent. of the land in such areas would come into national ownership in the first ten years.

The Hobhouse Committee showed considerably more awareness than Dower had done of the need for accessible situation in the areas selected for Parks, though the selection they actually made was not very different. To Dower, natural beauty was something sacred in itself, irrespective of how many or how few might benefit by it—in some ways indeed the fewer the better. Dwelling by her untrodden ways she was a maid whom there were few to praise and very few to love. In this sense his ideal could properly be described as a national one inasmuch as not specifically designed for the enjoyment of regular ramblers resident in particular con-urbations, or as a spiritual one inasmuch as not mainly concerned with practical convenience. The Hobhouse Committee, however, recognised that Parks were made for mankind, and at least examined their relation to the numbers of people who could reasonably be expected to make use of them, not merely on an annual holiday but at week-ends. Parks, after all, however national the intention, could not be other than local in their *clientèle*. Failure to appreciate this would seem to introduce a fallacy into the reasoning of those who, like Trevelyan, thought modern city life only tolerable on condition of frequent and deep draughts of nationalised nature—for how could anyone who felt thus about the place where he lived and worked endure it at all if he could only hope, like Browning's Pippa, or Matthew Arnold's Judas Iscariot, to escape from it once a year? But the hard facts of geology still continued to locate the romantically wilder parts of Britain mainly in the west and north. Ellemess, the dark-tressed oread, austerely beckoned from the mist-clad heights haunted by the spirits of the bards, whilst her blonde sister Ellenee indulged in less edifying jinks at places like Skegness.

On the question of control, Sir Arthur Hobhouse's committee were considered, by the advocates of National Parks, to be sound. The new Parks were to be preserved from the control of the elected local authorities, by a recommendation that on each Park Authority the members (including the chairman) to be nominated by the National Parks Commission should in effect be in a majority of one over the members representing local authorities. The selection of areas disregarding existing county and district boundaries, together with the well-known cumbrousness of the device of joint boards which was thereby made necessary, would have the effect of further dividing and weakening the local representation and of rendering popular influence more ineffective. This distrust of democratic government seems to have been directed as much against counties such as Lancashire, from which would come most of the townspeople for whose enjoyment such a National Park as the Lakes would in fact cater, as to those such as Westmorland, the greater part of whose area was to be within the Park boundaries and the populace of which was to provide the spectacle of rustic life for the enjoyment of the visitors. Although 'the countryman is the true landscape gardener' he was not to be trusted with the governance of his home area any more than were the urban masses at whom Wordsworth had looked down his nose.

At a later date this recommendation was the subject of a stiff battle in the House of Commons Select Committee on the National Parks Bill, and the Act finally provided that the proportion of the membership to be appointed by the Minister, on the nomination of the National Parks Commission, should form up to one-third only of each local Park Board. It is doubtful whether the Minister (as he indeed admitted) could easily have found enough persons suitable as well as willing to act, if the proportion had been fixed higher than this.

The National Parks and Access to the Countryside Act, 1949, was passed in December of that year. The Commission had then to be set up and staffed, and the boundaries of proposed Park areas negotiated. The Commission's designation of the Lake District Park area, amounting to 866 square

miles, was confirmed by the Minister in May 1951. Slightly
more than half of this was in Cumberland, whilst the larger
part of what remained was in Westmorland and the rest in
Lancashire. The expression 'Lake District' was very liberally
interpreted, as its frontier was made to run well outside the
outer flanks of the main area of mountain country, and
extended to the boundaries of Penrith, Ulverston, Kendal,
Millom and Cockermouth. On the south, the frontier just
touched the heads of the estuaries of the Kent, the Leven,
and the Duddon, but took in a dozen miles of coast-line from
the boundary of Millom to the farther end of the sand-dunes
north of the Ravenglass estuary. The most notable single
alteration from the area originally proposed was the
exclusion of the little resort of Grange-over-Sands.

In fixing the representation of the three separate counties
on the Park Board, population as well as area had to be
considered. Of the 42,000 people in the area, some 18,000
were in Cumberland, 17,000 in Westmorland and 8,000 in
Lancashire. But Lancashire as a whole had far greater
financial resources than the other two, and supplied the
great bulk of visitors. It was therefore agreed between the
counties that each should contribute an equal share of the
ordinary administrative expenses and that their numbers
of representatives should be equal. Four were thus to be
appointed by each county, and to these twelve were added
six more, who were appointed by the Minister on the
nomination of the National Parks Commission.

It is not our purpose to explain fully the provisions of the
Act, but we ought to state briefly the way in which it may
affect the characteristics of the Lake District as we have
historically described them, and especially as it evidences a
change in the official attitude, and in the attitude of the
public, towards our subject. Since the Act has been in
operation, there has been some discussion as to whether the
interests of picturesque amenity are now to be regarded as
paramount over all other considerations, or not. The Lake
District National Park Board has, like all other local National

Park authorities, two main functions: It has the powers of a Planning Authority under the Town and Country Planning Acts, and also what are called 'management powers', which are additional to any powers possessed by a normal local authority, and which enable it to spend money on improvements (with the benefit of up to 75 per cent. government grant). The Planning powers are powers to approve applications for change of use of land (including building and the design of buildings) for all the purposes of ordinary life as well as for the purposes of the National Parks Act.

In introducing the Bill, on second reading, the Minister (Mr. Silkin) said:

> This is a small island, and we cannot afford, as in the United States, to set aside large areas solely for recreation or indeed for the purpose of establishing a museum. . . . I can give no guarantee that it may not be essential to permit a certain amount of 'undesirable development' in the national park areas; it may be necessary to permit some part of the area to be used for national defence; it may even be necessary to utilize the mineral wealth which lies in those areas to ensure the economic life of the people.

Since the passing of the Act, as well as before it, friends of the picturesque have, however, claimed more than this. Thus, Lord Strang, the Chairman of the National Parks Commission, has often remarked that 'there always had been, and always would be what is held to be good and sufficient reason' why the interests of amenity should sometimes give way to other national interests—his implication being that such reasons should be disregarded, notwithstanding their being good and sufficient.

The words of the Act itself (as they may be interpreted by the Courts) provide of course the final arbitrament between the diverging views represented by the pronouncements of the Minister and of Lord Strang. The Act, in conferring functions on the planning authorities, does not specifically dictate to them which proposals they shall allow to prevail in particular cases, no doubt because it is their duty to hold a balance on the particular facts, having regard, amongst all other considerations, to such general directions (if any) as are to be found in the Act. The nearest we get, in the Act, to an evaluation of its objectives is contained in section 5, which states that it is 'especially desirable' that measures shall be taken in the Act (as thereafter set out) for the purposes of the Act. These purposes are then described as 'preserving and enhancing' the natural beauty of the areas to become National Parks, and 'promoting their enjoyment by the public'. This seems to fall short of declaring that these purposes shall be absolutely 'overriding' or 'paramount', but amounts to saying that the multifarious machinery set up by the Act is intended to ensure that their especial desirability in any particular case shall receive serious consideration.

Pronouncements made from time to time by Ministers regarding the purposes of the Act (despite the respect which must be paid to them at the time) are only to be taken as representing temporary policy, for the Minister has no power to make definitive interpretations. We may say, therefore, that whilst there is nothing in the Act to give picturesque considerations a fixed or absolute degree of priority over other needs (many of them also of national importance) the actual degree of importance which will be attached to them either by the Park Planning Authorities or by the Minister for the time being will vary according to the merits of the particular case, and is unpredictable.

CHAPTER XXVI

CONCLUSION: A CASE OF SPLIT PERSONALITY?

ON ANY SHOWING, the passing of the National Parks Act must be a milestone. Fresh from the workshop of parliament, an Act is but a robot, a mechanical thing of clauses and provisos, unintelligible to the layman. Only by a phrase here and there will it echo the human hopes and struggles which have gone to its making—and such phrases usually are by no means the ones that will convey the clearest meaning to lawyers. The intentions of those who planned it are now totally irrelevant. What matters henceforth is not what the Hobhouse Committee wished or meant but what the Act says. The administration of any Act is, from the time of its passing, in this free country inevitably in the hands of many other people than those who sponsored it. But it is just the way that its new masters administer it which will, in time, furnish it with a living tradition, will graft it on to the life of the nation, and the robot seems to come to life.

It is too much to expect that such interpretation will always be sympathetic. Laws must be administered as they are written; they are not the private property of those who agitated for their enactment. But it is a necessary condition of the Act's working at all that some common point of view should be developed, for example between the members of any Park Planning Board, regardless of whether they have been appointed by the Minister or by the locally elected bodies. It is needless to stress the necessity for this, since it is quite certain that it will come about—in this country it always does. The Minister, the Courts, and the professional bias of administrators will all play their part. Partisan pressure from various sides may not be ineffective; but the habit of dealing in common with the practical necessities of case-work will be much more powerful, and any attempt to regard one section of the administrators as watchdogs against another section merely delays this process and lessens the authority of the governing body as a whole. Never, therefore, do we see the administrators of an Act of Parliament acting in the role of knights in shining armour, vowed singlemindedly to a cause.

The same principle of co-operation is needful as between agencies on different levels. By the Act, the central National Parks Commission is given considerable powers to 'make representations' to the Minister about the doings of the local Park Planning Boards in whose hands rests actual executive power, and to 'consult with' the latter (that is, to admonish them) and to 'report to the Minister' (which in ordinary language means to issue propaganda to the public). Even more than this was sought at the time of the consideration of the Bill, in Parliamentary Committee. But it was pointed out by the Minister that a power for a non-elective body to issue 'directions' to elective bodies, or partly-elective bodies (as the Park Boards were) was something for which there was not, nor could be, any precedent in English constitutional practice. Without taking too much time on this subject, one may remark that the very survival of all this machinery depends on these extensive powers being exercised in a spirit of moderation so as to enlist the co-operation of the resident public.

A weakness of Park legislation on the national scale is that the practical problems to be solved differ in almost every one of the Park areas. Occasionally, major archaeological features such as Hadrian's Wall may be the *raison d'être* of a Park, or the preservation of rare flora and fauna, although in the latter case Nature Conservancy control may be adopted in preference. In Cornwall or Pembrokeshire, a new coastal path may be intended. In some cases it may be desired to preserve an area which is felt to be unique or beautiful—not perhaps much threatened, but the attractiveness of which depends on some conjunction of natural and historical causes which it would be difficult to reproduce afresh. In other cases it may be necessary to regulate an area of open country—not outstandingly beautiful perhaps, but tightly sandwiched between urban concentrations, whose teeming millions need it as a playground and whose overspill of development threatens to swamp it. It may be necessary in some districts to guarantee access for the visitor in face of the exclusiveness of farmers or game-preservers, whilst in other districts it may be more necessary to protect the established users of land from being overrun by ill-behaved hordes of townspeople, or even to extend the latter's privileges in order to avert worse.

All these objectives are of course the legitimate subject-matter of planning; but administration under a general act may mean much more comprehensive control than would be thought necessary if the problems of one individual area only were under consideration, and may mean some steam-rollering of the special characteristics of individual Park areas. Prejudices and controversies which have hitherto been confined to certain parts of the country may possibly widen their scope, and infect other areas. Hitherto, for example, the aversion which some people feel towards forestry in the Lake District, has not apparently been felt by their opposite numbers in other parts of the country. The rash of caravan and shack encampments has been, at its worst, confined to the sea-side and has not formed part of the traditional method of enjoying the Lake District. The Lake District, too, has known nothing of the civil war of ramblers against land-owners and farmers which has been seen in the Peak. Even amenity societies have acknowledged that there is little need in the Lake District to do much in regard to the 'access' provisions of the Act; as the worsening of local relations which would result, would outweigh any benefit that could be secured. The same argument indeed might be applied to excessive zeal in regard to footpaths.

We can now consider the possibilities of successfully

planning such a district as ours through the agency of a National Park authority. From an orthodox picturesque point of view, the special charm of the Lake District does not lie solely in its wildness, but in other elements, which may of course seem important in different degrees to different people. There is the close contrast of natural wildness, with shelter, habitation, comfort, and even luxury. There is the assiduous management which, over five or six generations has harmonised these elements. There is the unobtrusive way in which most of this has been done; at one end of the scale the poverty of the soil has imposed its own discipline on human building and living, and it has been very much of a modern tradition to imitate the result. The individualism and idiosyncrasy of persons has also its attraction. There is the sense of seclusion, of each valley separately. To one cause at least the district certainly does not owe such charm as it can show: to large-scale planning by public authorities, however cautious, however 'safe'.

The Cumbrian poet, Norman Nicholson, has emphasised the basic causative force of the rocks underlying any district, how they set the pattern both of agriculture and of building, and, through these, the character of the people. So, apart from the three great bands of Skiddaw slates, 'Borrowdale' lavas, and Silurian slates, the central hills look down to areas of granite, of lowland sandstone, of limestone, of alluvium, and to the sea estuaries. These indications support the view that the Park area, administratively so unwieldy, should be divided into three parts at least. It is very curious, therefore, to find so much emphasis laid by the advocates of National Parks on the necessity for uniformity of administration over all parts of the area of the Park—over the parts which look north over the agricultural plain to the Border, westward to the Cumbrian industrial belt, eastward to the limitless Pennines, or south to the paths of the rain-bringing winds and of the mass invasions of tourists.

In the Lake District, right of access to the hills has hardly been a problem at all, and demand for private development has not reached a stage beyond the capacity of ordinary planning authorities to deal with. In marked contrast to parts of the Derbyshire Peak area, the harmonious relationship between visitor and native has itself in the Lakes been such as to contribute much to the charm of the district, and has been a tradition. Far more indeed has been heard here of conflict of temperament or interest between visitor and resident since the passing of the Act, than ever before.

In every Park, although in different proportions, the aim of preservation of one sort or another stands contrasted with the aim of opening up the area to the public. Which of these two aims will ultimately prevail over the other is a question as yet undecided. The earlier sponsors of the National Park movement—the right wing, as we may call them—were preservationist, and preservation has held the field up to now; but if the movement should ever be successful in attracting the warm support on the part of the public at large, on which its hopes were set, my guess is that this can only be on the basis of permitting much of the type of amusement that the Dower Report deprecated. The *pur-sang* preservationist may even come to regret the passing of the Act.

How much active interest, up to the present, does the man in the street take in all this? How has the establishment of National Parks affected the way he looks at the Lake Country? What, in their turn, are the administrators trying to make of the physical aspect of the country? How goes the post-statutory tradition-forming process we have mentioned?

To begin with the ordinary man, one gets the impression that he specifically cares very little whether his recreational areas are regulated as National Parks or not. Realising this, perhaps, although somewhat dimly, the enthusiast for National Park organisation calls for an extended use of propaganda, to make the ordinary man realise by whose grace it is that the sun shines on Skiddaw, that Helvellyn is not low nor Winander dry. A mystical distinction is drawn between 'mere regional parks' and National Parks. It is, frankly, no use my attempting to explain this distinction, as I have not succeeded in understanding it. The Hobhouse Committee clearly contemplated that the main users of each National Park would be the city-dwellers living nearest to it.

Regarding this mystical difference, Mr. James Fisher recently writes, in admission of the lack of spectacular achievement in National Parks so far, 'for goodness sake call them County Parks and leave them to get on with it, and forget the idea that we once had, as a nation that' (I omit here a catalogue of well known British tourist regions) 'are national treasures beloved in every corner of England and Wales.' But on the same page, complaining of the lack of sign-boards, advertisement and propaganda in National Parks, he says, 'I could not have told whether I was in a National Park or not.' Could he really have meant that the beauties of nature mean nothing to him unless they are suitably labelled? Apparently this was just what he did mean, for what sort of remedy does he go on to propose? 'What the National Parks Commission should provide is a *public face* to our National Parks movement. Just think of the difference if each of our Parks had noble headquarters, with information facilities . . . park museum . . . dioramas. . . .' The ordinary taxpayer might possibly not be so favourably impressed by the noble headquarters, and might care less than nothing whether the information, the museums, the side-shows provided are run by one set of people rather than another. What indeed is lacking is not money so much as creative ideas. Desirable as the details of such an educative or recreational plan may be, it requires the efforts of very many and very diverse people to fulfil it and there is really no reason why they should all fly one flag.

But when indeed did the man in the street have precise and decided ideas about subjects other than those of strictly practical utility? It is unfair to expect it. If we want express answers to our questions we must look to special classes: for example, the enthusiasts of the National Parks movement, or the dedicated fell-walkers, or the malleable and as yet un-dedicated young people for whom special holiday centres, hostels and mountain training centres are provided, or the professional planning administrators.

A tempting case to begin with is that of the recently established Mountain Training Schools such as the one in Eskdale. The parent impulse of these had not originally any-thing to do with the romantic sentiment of mountains, but the schools were the offspring of educational and social ideas. Their lineage is from pre-war educational experiments in Germany, via Gordonstoun in Moray and the Sea School at Aberdovey. Their watchword was integration in the life of their district, expressed in practical tasks of good neighbour-liness, such as coastguard work or life saving. As it happened, however, the men who have developed them in their later stages have been lovers of mountains too, and the mountains therefore are chosen as the arena in which the character-training, which is their essential purpose, is carried on. They do not exist to train mountaineers, as such, still less aesthetes, and indeed one sees no reason why their own worthy and sufficient object could not be carried on almost equally well in a Lake District full of the largest sizes of electric trans-mission towers, reservoirs, rocket-testing grounds or quarries (one does not, of course, suggest that this would be a positive advantage). Let us leave them, therefore, for the moment, but not forget their essential thesis, that the circumstances of civilised life to-day are deficient, at any rate in certain strata of society, or age-groups, in opportunities for the more heroic virtues.

In seeking to record the positive aesthetic ideas of the advocates or administrators of National Parks, this chapter might almost have resembled the famous one in Buffon's natural history entitled *The Snakes of Iceland*, which was very short, for there are no snakes in Iceland. One can indeed enumerate on the side of positive achievement such simple devices as telephone boxes painted grey with red edging, or by-law boards painted in green (somehow never quite like the green of any grass or leaf) or standardised advertisements for petrol stations which by their restrained uniformity make us suspect that we are never more regimented than when we think we are on holiday. But generally what one encounters is a set of rather tiresome shibboleths of negative character. The emphasis is on preservation, as if something— the picturesqueness of the Lake District—had accidentally come about, which, although admittedly owing much to human as well as to natural agencies, was beyond the power of the conscious designer to better, reproduce. This is presumably accounted for by the argument that the picturesque arrangement of a Lake District farmhouse or village or farm, is the unconscious work of the local peasantry, inspired or guided by personified Nature. It follows from this Wordsworthian conception that the peasant should willy-nilly be protected against any influence which may distract or tempt him from his function.

Unfortunately, this aesthetic criterion very easily degenerates into the uncritical acceptance of whatever is familiar, or is associated with agreeable holidays. Phrases like 'the traditional Lakeland style' are used of what was never in its origin an artistic style at all; and admiration is extended to such matters as the architecture of the greater part of the central Lakeland villages, which, as architecture, are remarkable for little but nineteenth-century dullness, with much crudity in execution. Progress cannot lie this way, and, without progress, follow staleness, coma, and death.

It thus happens that the aesthetic standards which one is able to disinter from the propaganda of the enthusiasts turn out to be predominantly negative, and particular negative instances acquire great relative prominence. Such and such a place must not be used for industry; a proposed building is 'out of keeping with tradition'; forestry is disliked because it is 'commercial'. Wooden electric poles are consistently referred to as pylons, however many times the error

CONTEMPORARY USERS

may be pointed out.* Comparatively little welcome awaits active design, little need seems to be felt in that direction.

The author is persuaded that, whatever may be the case with picturesqueness, beauty cannot be purchased in ready-wrapped packets made up according to simple prescriptions, nor can it be ensured merely by the observance of a few simple taboos. The full enjoyment of beauty requires a keenness of mental attitude which is the antithesis of lazy sentiment. Some people's imaginations are naturally active; by others perceptivity is a matter of effort and attainment; others again, more insensitive, require the shock of novelty, wildness, danger, to awaken them. For these, wild landscape can render the service of a necessary jolt. But they are astray, if at this point they let themselves fall under the spell of a new set of shibboleths, which can only lead them to a position as sterile aesthetically as the town habitat they have left.

One would indeed think that anyone so blind, or mentally blind, as to be unable to tell a pylon from a wooden pole (or who was liable to confuse the style of certain local late-Victorian speculative builders with 'traditional' native building) would be disqualified from raising his voice in aesthetic controversies at all, but such is far from being the case. The light tenor note of aesthetic pleasure or pain is sustained by the deeper growl of, well, almost of moral feeling.

This gives us the key, perhaps to the enigma, of how is it that numbers of people whose caravans or cars and whose dress and personality bear very little evidence of personal artistic achievement or cultivated taste, should be so hypersensitive to such simple things as wooden poles, or the necessary use of simple materials such as corrugated iron roofing, concrete and so on in the after all very down-to-earth business of farming?

* There have never been any pylons in the Lake District, and I cannot remember when any have been proposed.

The things to which they object are not objected to on their own aesthetic demerits, but as symbols of social discontents. As all through our story, a certain number of townsmen can hardly see the country, fair or foul, except in reaction to their feeling about the place they permanently live in. This sort of Lake District enthusiast, when he visits his playground, does not wish to be reminded of the kind of town he has allowed to come into existence, or the century in which he lives. Hence the popularity of such novels as Hugh Walpole's *Rogue Herries* sequence; and hence the allergy to such things as electric power lines, however unimportant from a strictly aesthetic point of view. Hence the double standard of amenity for town and country respectively (with its curious unreality as regards the latter), evident in the Scott Report—a double standard which has persisted ever since, in romantic attitudes towards the planning of the Lake District.

But the works of mankind are not necessarily ugly in themselves, any more than the phenomena of nature are necessarily beautiful. Nature indeed offers us an enormous choice of sights and sensations, which serve us as the raw material of which we build our ideas of beauty which we express in works of art. But the music is in the musician, not in the wood and catgut of his instrument. The spirit of mountain enjoyment is in the climber, the artist or the naturalist, and not in the mindless rock or water. His eye and mind pick out what they need. The often-repeated comparison of a district of grand scenery to a valuable work of art is an utterly fallacious one. Besides, it is the museum administrator, the wealthy collector and his imitators, who hoard works of art—the artist prefers to create his own. We can all be artists, on however humble a plane. To get the best, we must be figuratively as well as literally on our toes, and if we are accustomed to making good use of what is before our eyes we can find beauty in a pebble, in the grimy texture of a paving-stone, in the varying colours of a heap of bricks. If we do not take the trouble to do this, we do not deserve to be believed when we claim that one thing is in itself more beautiful than another.

In the feeling, not exactly of horror or dread, but one akin to these, which they so often expressed, some of the eighteenth-century commentators, seeing our scenes with fresh eyes, were very right. Very many people to-day must feel much as they did, although it is our fashion to be shy of expressing ourselves with the same candour. So, from simple materials, labelled, in plain language, barren, harsh, lonely, arduous, poor, the mountain-lover may compose for himself pictures to which he gives such titles as adventure, meditation, heroism. Or again he may prefer to leave the picture without a title, though it is still a picture of his own making, one to which nature herself is indifferent. If, however, we rest content with the crude sense of the sublime, without exercising our faculties of imagination and of criticism, we do not get very far.

The artist's synthetising mind can use either fresh natural impressions, or materials of any kind washed clean of their old context, but many people find it much harder to use man-made fragments as the material of their own workshop of the imagination. Towns may not necessarily be ugly, but they may seem very stale. Unselfconscious utilitarianism, however, is not, aesthetically speaking, stale in the way that fragments of poor design, linked with outworn ideas, are so. A quarry, a farm, a reservoir barrage, even a railway, is not likely to be ugly in itself in the way in which a suburban building layout, or the design of the frontage of a cinema may be. For in the one case, the panorama of life and work has its essential dignity, and the great efforts of industry their sublimity even; whilst in the other, perhaps, a designer not of the first rank has left them smeared with the imprint of his personality, or a well-meaning committee has trimmed and clipped them in the effort to apply some battered collection of accepted rules, begotten of compromise and muddle out of slogan.

These remarks perhaps open up views upon questions

P

rather too wide to be fully dealt with in this book. But the problems of the English conurbations, and of that part of our civilised habitat which we still choose to call the country-side, are essentially similar. It is for all of us that the bell tolls, in our homes, our workshops, on our arterial roads, in our cars and in our caravans. Our holiday haunts do but hold the mirror up to us, as we are; let us take courage to look. If this is the sort of people we are, what is lost by admitting it? If we do not care to think so, let us give proof of it where we live.

One certainly does not deny the need for facing the problems of planning, in the country as well as in town, and for patiently building up a technique which will enable us to hold an even balance between our various needs, as well as between our needs and our ideals. It is not, however, by grandiose legislative and bureaucratic programmes, but by accepting personal responsibility for our principles, especially in the centres where we work and live, that we shall achieve serenity. Only by personal cultivation of our aesthetic faculties can we achieve stable aesthetic foothold—only by remedying both social and aesthetic evils in the places where they are most intense, shall we deliver ourselves from our neuroses about towns.

Objections to the normal planning for modern life in National Park areas may of course inflict hardship or in-justice on the people who live there. A stronger criticism of such objections is that they make nonsense of the standards under which the objectors are content to live, in their own homes. If we cannot bear when on holiday to be reminded of what we are and where we live, then there must be much that is avoidably wrong with our way of life, and we should set about putting it right. There is no escape from this conclusion, however awkward it may be to recognise it. England is much too small, much too socially unified, for it to be possible to set up alongside each other two entirely different standards of taste, of planning, and of the basic social and economic organisation on which they would respectively have to rest. But if we recognise this, avoiding romanticism and snobbery, we may find that we have built as well as the men of old, and be free to enjoy, both in and out of National Parks, the beauty and picturesqueness of common things.

MAN AND EARTH

So, Fingal in the peat-moss stooping darkly
Burdens the lucent rill with his hot shadow;
Hunted by thirst, by thirst of heart, the hunter
Slips from his shoulder, casts where he cares not, quickly,
The carcase all day hunted; hunted is he now
By vast oppression of the empty heavens,
Bayed by life's mocking silence;
Hearkens asudden where the mosses whisper,
Where low the water speaks
Under stones wordless—
Save what words can show
Time's silly vassal, this
Hurrying biped, heir of creation, show him
Agelong metamorphosis and the speechless march of seasons.
Drink here, lost Fingal when a thousand years
Have filled your land with church-bells;
So, when, still,
The sultry peat-moss cowers in the heat
Of summer, through eventless days,
Stoop, in your hundredth grandson's changeless gesture, when
The strange new gods are fallen again.

INDEX